IN THEIR OWN WORDS

BOYZONE

BOYZONE...IN THEIR OWN WORDS

Exclusive distributors:

Book Sales Limited
8-9 Frith Street, London W1V 5TZ, UK

Music Sales Corporation
257 Park Avenue South, New York, NY 10010, USA

Five Mile Press
22 Summit Road, Noble Park, Victoria 3174, Australia

Exclusive distributors to the music trade only:

Music Sales Limited
8-9 Frith Street, London W1V 5TZ, UK

ISBN 0.7119.7915.4
Order No. OP48167

Compilation and introduction by Seamus Riley

All photographs supplied by LFI

Edited by Chris Charlesworth

Cover and Book designed and originated by **Hilite**

Picture research by Nikki Lloyd, Omnibus Press

Special thanks to Ian Welch for research assistance

Every effort has been made to trace the copyright holders of
the photographs in this book but one or two were unreachable.
We would be grateful if the photographers concerned would
contact us.

Printed in Great Britain by Page Bros Ltd, Norwich, Norfolk.

Visit Omnibus Press at
www.omnibuspress.com

OMNIBUS PRESS

A video clip of Boyzone dancing on an Irish TV chat show just after their late-1993 formation is a much-repeated staple of Before They Were Famous-style programmes. But that's purely because everything the talented quintet have touched since appears to have turned to precious metal. No group can match their unbroken record of Top 5 singles, and while other boy bands like Take That, 911 and Bad Boys Inc have failed to stay the course Ronan, Mikey, Shane, Steve and Keith have remained unassailable.

Yet their own individual lives have changed beyond recognition - and not just in fame terms. Three of them are now fathers, while Stephen Gately has confirmed the widely circulating rumours of his homosexuality. Yet though such things could once have been thought turn-offs to a predominantly female audience, Boyzone's record sales and stature have remained at previous levels, if not actually increased. The only danger to their continuing domination of the boy-band scene would seem to be themselves; with

Ronan Keating developing parallel careers as a TV show host and chart-topping solo singer, the odds are that the five individuals will opt for their own paths sooner if not later.

But with plans for the new millennium that include a new album, tours and a biographical film, the Boyzone juggernaut shows no sign of grinding to a halt just yet - even if more time will be factored in for family responsibilities. This book lets them tell their story so far, covering their own relationships both within and outside the band, the effects of fame and their growing interests in non-musical pursuits. Even non fans who've observed the phenomenon from afar will find some eye-opening opinions as the sayings of Boyzone offer us a privileged peek into their world.

In The Begining
The lads' childhood years pre-Boyzone

I wouldn't say my upbringing was strict, we just knew our place. We knew when to say things and when not to. Obviously I was bold, every child is bold, and I did naughty things. I can't say I was the perfect child. Then again we weren't wild. We had a very Catholic upbringing. My mum particularly is a very religious woman and she's brought us all up to be very religious too. I try to spend as much time as possible in church.
Ronan

I was lucky because all of my childhood was excellent, but the worst thing that I can remember was getting up for school in the morning!
Shane, January 1995

When I was about 12, I'd been having really bad headaches and I had to go into hospital for a load of tests. They didn't find anything wrong but I had to stay in for a week. I hate hospitals, too - can't stand them. I couldn't eat the food, so people smuggled in lots of sweets for me.
Ronan

I used to look at New Kids on the Block posters when I was about 11 and say to myself that someday I'd be like them. I also thought about girls having my picture on their walls and fancying me.
Shane, June 1995

I was always known in my family as 'Little Ro'. At least it meant I was very spoilt especially on my birthday and when Christmas came around. I was very close with my eldest brother Ciaran even at that time, and he'd always protect me from the others. Gary and I really got on too. He was five years older and I wanted to do everything he was doing.
Ronan

(TV) influenced me when I was younger. I watched Zorro when I was eight or nine and decided I'd like to leave a mark everywhere like him. I cut a triangle shape in everything - curtains, cushions, you name it. I said one of my mates had done it, but I was found out and bashed for it.
Keith

I always used to think I was a superhero. I thought I was Superman for a while, then it was Spiderman. I used to climb trees and then fall off. I broke my arm about six or seven times! I never had an imaginary friend, but some people have to.
Ronan

I didn't like my first teacher. She always used to grab me by the ears when I was naughty in class.
Mikey, June 1995

When I went to a new school in the country some of the boys didn't like me 'cos I was from Dublin. They ganged up on me but I sorted them out. That was my first big fight.
Ronan, June 1995

My first job was at a golf driving range. I was 14, and we used to pick up all the balls. I saved up and bought myself a mountain bike.
Keith, June 1995

I started working part-time at my dad's garage when I was 14, then I did an apprenticeship. I think he respected my decision to leave school because he knew I hated it.
Shane, June 1995

My father is my idol. I think he's

I started writing songs in my first year in secondary school in English classes. I had melodies in my head.
Ronan, July 1996

My mother didn't want me to leave (school) and neither did my father. I didn't really persuade them I just did it. I had to take my own life in my hands.
Ronan, July 1996

When I was really young, I used to go and stay at my grandparents' house at weekends. I remember one time they let me stay up late and watch the movie 10, because they didn't realise it was a dirty film. I just remember sitting on the sofa, wearing my Super Ted pyjamas

I used to be very quiet -
I mean really quiet - and then
I took up acting and it was good
for me. It made me come out of
my shell a lot more and be
more outgoing.
Stephen, September 1996

I've known Keith for about
14 years. I can't remember the
first time I met him, but an early
memory I have of him is once
when I was walking by where
his road is and I was absolutely
covered in muck and I was
pushing a motorbike. I
remember Keith coming down
these steps that came down
from his road. He was dressed
in all blue denim - blue jeans,
blue shirt and he was shining!
He was just so clean from head
to toe and I was covered in mud.
Shane, 1996

I must have been about
five. We used to live in a block
of flats and I slept in the same
room as my sister and
brothers, apart from Tony who
was just a little baby. I woke up
in the   middle of the night and
couldn't hold on any longer - I
just had to see if Father
Christmas had come and left
presents under the tree. So I
woke up my brothers and
sister and we all crept into the
living room. It was so brilliant
to see all the gifts there. But
we were very good and
somehow managed to go back
to sleep…at least until 5am, at
which point we woke our
parents and told them we were
going to open our presents, so
they'd better get up and out
ofbed too.
Stephen, December 1996

I don't feel I have any amazing ambition of great focus - I had no idea that Boyzone was going to happen, no masterplan, I just knew I wanted to perform and worked hard at every aspect of what I do.
Ronan, January 1997

I was on holiday in Portugal with my family when I was about 15, and I downed too much cheap shandy booze. I ended up spending the night on the beach under an upturned boat!
Shane

I remember when (my first kiss) happened - I was 13 and she knew exactly what she was doing, but I didn't have a clue and it scared the life out of me. I can't even remember her name - some irst kiss!
Ronan, February 1997

I always wanted to do something with my life that was in the public eye, whether it be sports or entertainment. I was in a few rock bands before and I got the taste of it and wanted more. Once I got that taste it just grew and grew.
Ronan, March 1997

Until I joined Boyzone I was never very dedicated to anything. I hated school, I was a bit of a wild one. The only thing that ever held my interest was drama. That's why I knew I had to join Boyzone - it was like fate calling at my door. Until I joined the group, the highlight of my career as a performer was directing a play and playing a donkey in a Nativity play.
Ronan, September 1997

We used to laugh at nude pictures when we were younger. We'd giggle in school when the teacher started talking about sex and passing round books with rude pictures in. You never really grow out of sniggering at rude things do you? I think it's really important to laugh at things like that.
Stephen, September 1997

You have to work hard for what you want in life. I remember me dad telling me how, when my eldest sister Tara was born, he hardly saw her or me mam for three years. He was working all hours setting up his own business and would be out of the house from six in the morning until one o'clock the next morning. My mam would get out of bed to make him dinner, he'd have a quick kip and then go back to work. After he explained that to me, I could never imagine complaining about working hard.
Shane, October 1997

I'm not usually a jealous type of person but when I was growing up my younger brother's birthday was on May 15 and my elder brother's birthday was on May 17 so they'd get presents, and cards, and money from all angles and I'd be left out. My dad was in the rag trade, though, so he'd bring me a couple of tops as a little surprise.
Keith, September 1998

I used to stay in the house with just my brother when I was about 11. I was very nervous in the house without me mam and dad. I was up the walls with worry. I used to go to bed with a hurling stick, a golf club and a carving knife under my pillow. My brother still slags me for it.
Keith, September 1998

I used to sign my name in the (school) roll for days when I wasn't in. I'd Tipp-Ex out the crosses and put ticks so it looked like I had a really good attendance.
Stephen, November 1998

As much as I want my son to have a stable background and schooling and things like that, I also want him to travel around the world and learn to be street-wise. While there was nothing wrong with my childhood, I never left Ireland until I joined the band at 16. I'd just like my child to try the food of the world and to meet different people from different cultures. Because it's a wonderful world out there.
Ronan, December 1998

Loads of people laughed at me when I dropped the collection box once (in church). I was about 13 and the priest was saying Mass, which of course is a very serious, quiet time - and I dropped the box! All the money dropped out and rolled around the floor - I had to crawl around on me hands and knees to pick it up with everyone looking and laughing at me.
Stephen, April 1999

At 14, I signed autographs for people, saying I'd be famous. I always just wanted to get out of the rough areas of Dublin and the poverty of my childhood. We got by but my dad was a painter-decorator and my mum a housewife. Nobody pointed me in this direction and I'm proud of myself for doing it.

I've worked for what I've got. I can now give my parents everything they want and I'm very close to all my family. I don't think I could ever leave Dublin though - I love the atmosphere.
Stephen, May 1999

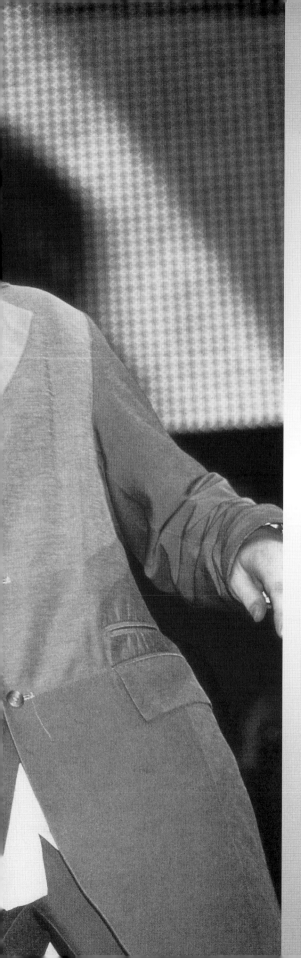

Not a lot of people know this, but I went to an all-girl primary school! I wouldn't say this is my greatest moment, but my most embarrassing was in art class. One day the teacher tried to make me wear an apron so I wouldn't spill paint on my clothes. I started crying because I thought it was a dress! I thought they were trying to turn me into a girl.
Shane, June 1999

All I ever wanted to do was make something of myself - and now I have.
Ronan, July 1999

As a child, I wanted to be up there on the silver screen. I loved Clint Eastwood, Al Pacino, John Wayne. All the he-men.
Ronan, July 1999

I was spoiled by my mother. My siblings all accepted it. They didn't mind - God, no. They knew I was the baby. I was her baby,
  My father was mostly out of the family working. He didn't show us his love, he was used to doing his own thing. I had all the love I needed from my mother.
Ronan, July 1999

I grew up in a rough part of Dublin and our family didn't have much money so occasionally I'd sneak onto the bus without paying. I wouldn't advise it though, no matter how skint you are, 'cause you'll have to pay twice as much when you get caught!
Stephen, August 1999

I'm really into films, and so when I
was too young to see a movie, I'd
lie and say I was older to try and get
into the cinema. Mind you, most of
the time, I still got turned away
because I'm quite small and
people didn't usually believe me.
Stephen, August 1999

Getting It Together
Boyzone's formation and their early path to fame

When I was offered Boyzone, all I wanted was to be able to leave school, to be honest. I hated it that much. I wanted so much for my mam to say, 'Yes, you can leave school.' But of course she didn't want me to leave. That was hard because I needed my mam's approval - I wouldn't have left if she hadn't come around to the idea. At the beginning she didn't know what her teenage son was getting into. She was scared, thinking the music business was all drugs and drinking.
Ronan

We're here to put even more sex back into pop because there's never enough, is there? And there's never been a pop group from Ireland. Ever. We're the only ones who've been brave enough. We've got the guts.
Keith, November 1994

We were on TV the day after we were picked. We had no routine, no choreographer and we weren't even friends! We were pathetic.
Ronan, November 1994

There just wasn't enough food to go around and the early mornings were also getting us down. But you just have to get on with it and put the bad times behind you because the good times far, far outweigh them.

When we moved into the house in London it was the first time most of us had been away from our parents. We were given £100 for the housekeeping which we spent down the supermarket, although we probably bought far too many biscuits and cakes.

But it was the state of the house that eventually got to us the most. You should have seen what a tip we'd turned it into after just three weeks living there! We never did any housework. I think the washing-up only got done twice. There were takeaway cartons all over the place, mixed in with smelly socks and clothes everywhere.

I was ashamed to invite anyone in. It was a complete dump by the time we moved out. It's probably better that we stay in hotels in the future.
Ronan, January 1995

Appearing on *Top Of The Pops* was amazing! It was a very long day and we spend most of the time in our dressing room but there were quite a lot of rehearsals. It's completely different to what you see at home on the telly. The studio is a lot smaller than it looks, which was quite disappointing, but we can't wait to do it again!
Stephen, January 1995

The Boyzone auditions were nerve-wracking. I remember seeing all these blokes there and thinking, 'I haven't a chance in the world'.
Stephen, June 1995

I wasn't disappointed when I was turned down initially for Boyzone; I had a feeling that it would be okay. So when one of the original members left, I was fairly happy to be called back.
Mikey, June 1995

When I left school I worked in Makullas clothes shop in Dublin. That was two months after I joined the band. People recognised me and I think fan mail's still sent there!
Stephen, June 1995

It's happened so quickly that none of us have really had time to take it all in. A year ago I was still messing around with cars in the garage and Ronan and Steve were still at school.
Mikey, June 1995

I cut my index finger on my right hand in the band's early days. I've been wearing a plaster on stage ever since. It's my lucky mascot.
Ronan, March 1996

When Keith walked in (to the auditions) I felt like walking out cos I didn't think I would get in. He had great clothes on and he was tall - and I just thought I'm not going to get in because I'm so small and weedy!
Stephen, 1996

I couldn't believe it when I found out we'd won (Best New Act on the *Smash Hits* Roadshow). It was just so brilliant. I think I had tears in my eyes on stage - I felt that emotional. It was just out of this world!
Ronan, July 1996

When we came over here two years ago, everybody saw us as just another boy band trying to cash in. But we did our own thing in interviews and made sure to get our own identities across. A lot of manufactured acts are told what to do, where to go and not to go out with certain people, but that has never applied to us.
Ronan, November 1996

We never thought it would happen so quickly. However, if 'Love Me For A Reason' had gone in at

Number 1, it wouldn't have done us any favours - we would have had to constantly follow that.

Thank God the whole thing progressed with the singles staying around the Top 5. We see the success of 'Words' as respect and recognition that we're not a flash in the pan.
Ronan, November 1996

I was very naive in the beginning and I had an awful lot to learn, but I was willing to grow so I kept my ears open, listened to everyone and never said a bad word about anyone. It's a lot different maturing in this business than maturing in college, believe me! If I was still in Dublin I'd probably be doing a 9-5 job now. I know I would have been content had I stayed, but

now I'm with the band I've seen there's so much more out there.
Ronan, January 1997

I've always wanted to do this. My life is dedicated to this. I wanted to be famous, I wanted to be in the limelight.
Stephen, October 1997

Because we didn't really know the business when we first started we might have been branded as one of these groups who aren't talented. We did silly things in TV shows for a laugh then regretted it because people assumed we were just another manufactured band.
Keith, September 1998

I wouldn't change a thing. We made the mistakes and we learnt from them, and that's why we're here today. We didn't make that many mistakes, but the ones we did make, we learnt from.
Ronan

We toured all around the Irish nightclubs, working from 6.00am until midnight. They were mad days and they really helped to make what we are today. But deep down we're still the same people we always were.
Ronan, May 1999

I am nostalgic for the time we spent touring round in a transit van. When we were unknown. It was so different then and we didn't know if we'd ever make it. That was very special.
Ronan, July 1999

The Music
Comments on the albums and singles

'Working My Way Back To You'
We released 'Working My Way Back To You' in Ireland. It entered the chart at Number 2 and stayed there. We now hate the song!
Ronan, July 1996

I wanted to sing lead, yeah, but I don't think I was jealous of Mikey and Stephen really. It just made me realise that I did want to sing, so I was lucky to get the second single.
Ronan, March 1997

'Love Me For A Reason'
The success of the record has been just brilliant. It's such a high when you go on shows alongside East 17 and Take That.
   But we haven't got two pennies to rub together. It makes us laugh when we go home and everyone says we must be millionaires.
Stephen, January 1995

We weren't disappointed about it not going to Number 1 because it meant that we could release 'Key To My Life' without too much pressure.
Ronan, July 1996

This put Boyzone on the map, but because we've done it five hundred million times I'm fed up with it. But it's a good song, it did the job.
Mikey, May 1999

'Key To My Life'
After 'Love Me For A Reason' there was a lot of talk about releasing another cover version. I suppose it would have guaranteed us chart success, but we said we didn't want to do that.
   We know we've got a lot to prove with this song. We have to convince people that we are good in our own right.
Shane, March 1995

The first song penned by Boyzone, for Boyzone. An okay song, interesting video. We were schoolboys in it. It was embarrassing, but it was done so well we couldn't really complain.
Mikey, May 1999

'So Good'
Not a bad song, but we had this particular dance routine to it that we absolutely hated. It involved jumping around like eedjits.
Mikey, May 1999

Said And Done
It's a great title because we've done everything we said we would.
Keith, June 1995

'Father And Son'
The beginning of us getting to a more mature sound. These lyrics mean a lot to me. They're about a

father trying to direct his son in life, and the son tells him to, er, bluff off. When you're young you think you know everything, but when you grow up you realise that you don't. The video? We just went along with it. At the time I thought it was okay, but now when I look at it I think, 'What was that about?'
Mikey, May 1999

'Coming Home Now'
'Coming Home Now' was our first single of the year and it was

special 'cause we did the video on the streets of Dublin - we had a right good laugh doing it and all the people were lovely. We had loads of kids out on the street messin' around and we even had all these mothers coming out from their houses and saying, 'D'youse want a cup of tea, lads?'
Ronan, 1997

In the end the single got to Number 1 in Ireland and Number 4 in the British charts

and I think we were all a bit disappointed about how it did - we expected a bit more from it.
Stephen, 1997

We'd been away from Ireland for a while so we decided to write this song. It was all right… not super dooper, you know?
Mikey, May 1999

'Words'
People blame us for the time we've been away and for the fact we're releasing a cover. They don't realise the record company or managers have their say, too.
 Obviously, people are gonna say, 'Another cover version?' But what's wrong with a cover? People can sing along better. The single after this, 'A Different Beat', will tell all - it'll show we can write our own stuff.
Ronan, October 1996

We had our first Number 1 this year with 'Words' - I think it's all part of a big masterplan that somebody up there's looking after. We hit

Number 1 just at the right spot - it was the first song from our second album and I think there's a good run ahead for us.
Mikey, 1997

We were happy to do it but it wasn't our choice. It's not what we wanted but what can you do? That's the way it is and, please God, people will still respect us and keep buying our records.
Ronan, special

When we used to do it live I'd get a great lift, but if you're doing it all the time you stop getting the emotional highs. Another cover? We weren't happy, but the powers that be decided that it was for the better. We put our foot down a lot more now.
Mikey, May 1999

'A Different Beat'
Good to do live - the audience love it. We did the video in a studio in London, but then they superimposed shots from Kenya so it looked like we went there. Some people said, 'Yeah, we were in Kenya for the video.' I'm telling you here and now, we weren't. We were working too hard at the time.
Mikey, May 1999

A Different Beat (Album)
When you listen to it, you'll see that we've progressed. We've matured within our image, our music and our attitude.
   It's nail-biting, 'cause we don't know what people will think of the new album. Obviously, the first album was Number 1, so this one has to be Number 1, too.
Ronan, October 1996

the first Number 1 record we'd written ourselves. And 'No Matter What' really opened doors for us all over the world, too!
Ronan, June 1999

I think individually we all have songs that are personal to us, songs that we particularly like. As a group though, there are also songs that we all agree are big favourites. 'Isn't It A Wonder' is a song we all agree on, definitely. We went over to Australia to shoot the video for that record which had a really good vibe.
Keith, 1999

'Picture Of You'
When we were filming the video. Mr Bean blew up our car and the burning smell reminded me very much of that Hallowe'eny, bangers

I think this album is definitely the next level for us. I'm hoping the song 'A Different Beat' will do for us what 'Back For Good' did for Take That. Boyzone have grown up a lot - we've all changed from boys to men since our first album. Hopefully people will respect us for these new songs.
Ronan

'Isn't It A Wonder'
Lovely song, and we had a great time making the video in a place called Broken Hill in Australia.
Mikey, May 1999

'Isn't It A Wonder' was the first song I wrote and I was very proud of that 'cause it was a bit of a turning point for me. 'A Different Beat' was a turning point for Boyzone as a band, 'cause it was

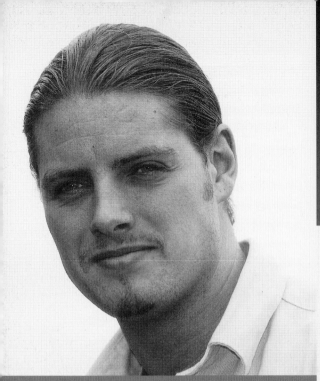

ladies in our videos and I prefer it when we do. It makes a change from looking at our ugly mugs. How much money did Tracy Chapman make from it? I've no idea. I don't know how much we got for it, never mind her.
Mikey, May 1999

smell from when I was little! It made me feel soppy and nostalgic.
Stephen, June 1997

The video was a laugh, that's what humour is all about, it was done very well, it's very classy and we're dead proud of it!
Ronan, October 1997

Great song, one of my favourites. A good, uptempo vibe. As we've gone on, we've done more and more ballads and I'm getting fed up of them now. I think we're going to have to start doing some fast songs.
Mikey, May 1999

'Baby Can I Hold You'
Tracy Chapman's old hit. A beautiful song. I enjoyed making the video. It was individual shots, so it only took about two hours. The girls in it were good as well. It had been a while since we'd had

'All That I Need'
Initially, I didn't like this song and I disagreed with it being a single. It reminded me of a typical American boy band - all swingbeat. But slowly it grew on me and it became Number 1. A few of the guys felt the same as me, though.

Mikey, May 1999
Where We Belong (Album)
It will be different (to the first two

albums) but that's because it's important to progress. Otherwise if you stay on the same level you come to a standstill fairly quickly. However, there will still be some pop songs on there because we are a pop band.
Mikey, June 1997

We would never rip anyone off! We re-released the album with two extra tracks because there was a demand. Obviously, people who bought it wanted to buy it. They could have waited for the next single, 'I Love The Way You Love Me'. There was no plot to rip people off.
Stephen, October 1998

'No Matter What'
There's still loads we want to do as

a band and there's loads that I want to do as a solo artist, but that's for the future - I'm not worrying about that yet. I think a lot has changed for us since the success of the last single. I mean, we've been going a long time now, but I'd look upon 'No Matter What' as being our first really massive hit. It's opened up a whole new audience for us, young and old. There's still a lot of work to be done, there's no doubt about that. There are loads of things we want to achieve and everyone's really up for it again.
Ronan, October 1998

I wasn't too sure about it at first. I thought maybe it might be a bit too soft for Boyzone, but I liked it after a few listens.
Mikey, May 1999

'I Love The Way You Love Me'
Ronan loved this song and

basically went away and recorded it until it was perfected for use with Boyzone. Did we mix up the first lines about kissing? No, it meant that the sound of a kiss and the feel of her name is the softest, most feminine thing about a woman.
Mikey, May 1999

'When The Going Gets Tough'
It was a joint decision. It was presented to us with a number of other songs and we thought, 'Why not?' It fits the (Comic Relief charity) cause, really. I actually remember it from the first time round and I watched the original video last night.
Stephen, April 1999

A great song for a great charity - we were honoured that we were asked to do it. Had it been a Boyzone song, it wouldn't have been chosen, but we did a good version. Billy Ocean was a great guy as well. The dance routine? Well, there wasn't too much movement, so it didn't bother me.
Mikey, May 1999

I thought it was a fantastic song. I wasn't too sure about us doing a version of it, but it's really grown on me.
Keith, 1999

It's one of those really uplifting party songs and we were just glad to be involved.
Ronan, 1999

By Request (Greatest Hits Album)
All in all, when I look at 'By Request', the only criticism I would have is that there are way too many covers. It annoys me - I mean, you might as well get Michael Bolton to sing them all. That aside, it's a good album - one of the best Greatest Hits albums around. Every track has been a hit and if you buy it you'll know all the songs.
Mikey, May 1999

It's strange! We have to pinch ourselves every now and then. A greatest hits album - it's fantastic! You have to put new tracks on as it sells the album, basically. The fans need an incentive to buy it as they'll probably have all the singles already!
Ronan, June 1999

It's unreal. It means we have come such a long way and that we're ready to move on to the next stage. It's like a new beginning - it's so exciting!
Shane, June 1999

'You Needed Me'
It's a love song, just what every man or woman would like to sing to their partner, innit?
Ronan, May 1999

That's an old song by a woman called Anne Murray. It means a lot too because it's a favourite of my mother's. She always sang it when I was growing up, so it reminds me of her.
Mikey, May 1999

The Winner Is...
How they've remained level-headed after awards and success

My family are delighted for me and they've told me to enjoy it while it lasts. When I go home they ask me how it's been going, I tell them, and then I have to go and do the dishes. My mates are the same. They tell me they saw me on the telly and, in the next breath, ask if we're all going out for a drink. So I'm very lucky in the respect that I have a lot of support back at home.
Shane, January 1995

Me and Mikey were in our hotel room when 'Love Me For A Reason' had just got into the charts and Mikey said, 'Keith, we're at Number 10' and we both just started laughing 'We're famous!' So no, it hasn't really sunk in. Everything is happening so fast we haven't had time to think about it.
Keith, January 1995

Being in this band is the chance of a lifetime and what we have achieved in the six months is absolutely brilliant.
  But our upbringing will keep our feet on the ground - we don't have time to act like something we are not. There are no egomaniacs in Boyzone.
Mikey, January 1995

I don't like being the big pop star. None of us do. I hate the way people act towards us sometimes, it's almost as if you're in a wheelchair or something, God forbid, but I don't need anyone to fetch and carry for me. I can hold my own bags.
Keith, April 1996

I wish I wasn't so hard now. It was so quick - I'd have liked to have grown up at my own pace, but it's

just something that comes with the job. Inside I'm quite hard, I can take a lot more than I used to. But I suppose it's quite a good thing not to be so naive. Naivety can cost you a lot in this business, and you have to be wise to get on.
Ronan, July 1996

This last year has been the hardest of my life. I switched off and blanked out everything in order to cope with what was happening in my life. The changes in my personal life were the most upsetting. You don't realise how valuable it is to be able to walk to the shops unnoticed. And then becoming a dad was something I can't even describe in words.
Mikey, July 1996

On tour I carry my own bags. At home I make my own bed, sweep the floor and still go down to the shops for me mam. I don't know, I guess I just try my best. It's not as hard as you might think - the only difference between me and another bloke my age is the job we do. I have a great job.
Ronan, July 1996

There are an awful lot of things that guys grow out of doing, like hanging round street corners and getting into trouble. It's all learning. We never had much time for getting into any trouble, fortunately, because it was all taken away from us.
Keith, August 1996

Losing my privacy has been a very big thing, but than it can be good to be recognised too. You learn to cope with it, and when I need to be alone I just go home.
Stephen, 1996

I'm still the same old Keith I always was - though if enough people say you've changed from time to time, you do start to believe them. My real friends tell me I've not changed a bit. I don't think I've turned into an idiot - even though I do act like one sometimes.
Keith, August 1996

We've seen other bands who started the same time as us get so big-headed, it's sad. I could've seen it happening to us but luckily we've kept each other in check the people around us (our families and manager in particular) have made sure our feet stay on the ground.

I still go home, go down the pub with my brother Ciaron, go down the shop with me ma, try to make the bed in the house - but not that often because I'm always in a rush to get a plane!
Ronan, January 1997

The thing that most annoys me is when the tabloids print rubbish about us, and about my private life. You know, journalists hide in my garden to sniff out stories. That annoys me, big time! Whenever they reckon they have a story about my personal life they camp outside, peer through my windows and try to get pictures of whatever they think might be going on. It's ridiculous.
Keith, June 1997

We encounter a lot of people who begrudge us our success because they're not doing as well, or whatever. I know it's part of the job and you have to expect it, but it still bothers me.
Ronan, October 1998

Obviously our lives have changed immensely since the band started, but we're not in any way starstruck.

We've all got very normal backgrounds and ordinary lives at home.
Keith, October 1998

We've been around for almost five years now, and I think we've taken everything in our stride, but what we've been trying not to do is believe the hype 'cos that's when it all goes very wrong. But we enjoy what we do and that's very important.

Fame hasn't taught me anything because I don't pay attention to it, you know? The job has taught me to open my eyes to everything and see what really goes on, 'cos we didn't know before the band. When we were living in Ireland we were living in our back garden and we didn't realise what went on out there. This business has made us grow up and pay attention to everything.
Ronan

The fame hasn't gone to my head or anything, but I certainly have changed a lot. I've tasted a much better life than the one I had before and I love it! Better food, fancy cars, money - these are all good things as long as they don't go to your head. The most important thing is to get along in life and never forget where you came from.
Ronan, October 1998

It's so flattering, being screamed at. As soon as that stops, that's when the whole thing ends, you know? Thank God we can still get people screaming at us.

In the past, we got a lot of grief for

The Beatles

being a boy band, but we've outgrown that and now people respect us. It's fantastic. Our next tour will be wild. It's sold out already, but I've no idea what it'll be like. Yet.

I've still got a lot left in me that I have to express. That'll come out in my later years when I find it easier to express myself, but I think I do a good enough job of it at the moment.

I do listen to my own records, but I don't gloat over them in any way. I learn from them, because I think it's important that you sing them better every time. Singing-wise, I think 'I Love The Way You Love Me' was my best performance yet - I'm just getting better and better. But, you know, there's always room for improvement.
Ronan, January 1999

they think? I don't need to answer to anybody I don't want to. I'm 23 years of age and I live my life by my own rules.
Stephen, May 1999

We are the PG Tips of pop - reliable and familiar. We're the only band besides Oasis and The Beatles to have had three consecutive chart-topping albums. We've had more Number 1 singles than U2. People forget that.

And who is to say The Beatles and Oasis aren't fans of Boyzone? There are a lot of people out there who wouldn't publicly say they were fans because of their image and our image. It makes me laugh. I'm sure even Liam Gallagher likes one of our songs.

And I don't think there is any real reason why we should split up, although some people would probably like us to. We always thought we couldn't get any bigger, but we did.
Mikey, May 1999

We were so naive when we started but we've learnt how to take care of ourselves and our business affairs. But we are not the multi-millionaires people think we are. We are still paying mortgages and stuff like that, although we're comfortably well off. I'm a millionaire approximately on paper but definitely not in my bank account.

I try to get money our of the hole in the wall if I can. That can be embarrassing when there are

I know, we're still here after six years. And finally getting recognition for our music. Winning an Ivor Novello Award (for songwriting) was really important to me. It's opened a lot of doors, and people respect me in a way they perhaps didn't before.
Ronan, February 1999

It's a very hard industry but I wouldn't know what else to do. It's in me blood now, I couldn't leave.
Ronan, May 1999

Sometimes I'll be walking along the street and people my age will start slagging me, and even older people actually. It really used to get to me, but now I look out for myself. Nobody else is going to live my life for me, so why should I care what

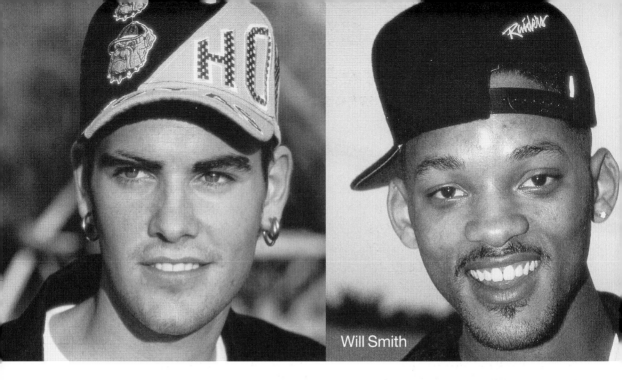

Will Smith

people there saying, 'Hey look, he's a superstar and he can't get any money out.'
It's all starting to fall into place now financially, but I count my blessings all the time.
Ronan, May 1999

Some newspaper journalists are just bitter towards us because from day one we couldn't give a monkey's about people who didn't like us. It would be great to accept loads of Brit Awards but… stuff 'em.
Shane, May 1999

Some interviews can be boring, some can be hard, but it's the only way to get the message across.
Ronan, August 1999

It's funny, actually, because as soon as you become famous you seem to get loads of stuff for free, even though by then you can actually easily afford it. I do quite a lot of stuff for Disney and so I get tons of free Disney toys and videos which is brilliant.
Stephen, August 1999

We've proved everyone wrong, haven't we? Six years ago everyone slated us. Now with three Number 1 albums and 16 hit singles we don't have to prove anything to anyone any more.
Ronan, August 1999

I've only lost my temper once with a photographer in all the years I've been in Boyzone. It was when we were leaving TFI Friday just after Ronan and Yvonne had baby Jack. This photographer obviously wanted to get a picture of the baby and he just barged into everyone and started pushing Ronan and me out of the way to get to Yvonne who was holding Jack. He was being really rough, so I shouted at him.
Stephen, August 1999

Boys' own Heroes
The people they admire whose example has kept them going

It's an honour to be compared with Take That. If we get half the success they've had I think we'd be chuffed to bits. There's no point in denying that they're an inspiration to us.
Ronan, June 1995

Will Smith is the reason I'm in Boyzone today. Seeing him in The Fresh Prince Of Bel Air got me interested in music.
Shane, June 1997

I'd love to meet Michael Jackson to see what he's really like, to actually sit down and have a chat with him. And I'd love to meet Janet Jackson, too.
Stephen, October 1997

I'll tell you who I really respect - All Saints. They've done brilliantly.
Shane, January 1998

Michael Jackson

George Michael is someone I'm still in awe of, but he's now a friend of mine. We talk on the phone and he sent Yvonne and me flowers for the baby. Bono from U2 is a wonderful person, too. There are few superstars in this business, and I'm lucky enough to know a couple of them.
Ronan, May 1999

My all time fave singer has to be Sting.
Mikey, June 1999

I need to make a name for myself as a solo act first off. I'd like to work with Shania Twain and Gary

Sting

George Michael

Barlow, and it'd be a total honour to sing with Elton John and George Michael!
Ronan, August 1999

I was totally speechless when I first met Michael Jackson - I've admired him for so many years and I just couldn't think of what to say - so I just stared at him. I reckon he must have thought I was totally mad! I met him again recently, when we played at his Michael Jackson & Friends concert and I managed to act a bit cooler then.
Stephen, August 1999

The Live Zone
Their attitude to performing and touring

I initially thought I'd be crazy to go on tour (so soon after suffering a broken leg), but fortunately I was talked into it. I decided to just get on with it. However, in Glasgow, I landed too hard on my sore leg. I was in absolute agony, but I couldn't scream because I had the headset mic on. So I just bit my lip and held it all in until the end of the song when I hobbled off the stage, took off the mic and let out a huge roar. What a relief that was!
Shane, September 1995

I jumped the wrong way and landed too near the edge of the stage. Whoomph! My leg went right through! I pulled it out and carried on as if nothing had happened, with a bright red face. Ronan kept looking over and laughing. It was very difficult to keep a straight fact, I can tell you.
Keith, September 1995

After the (Portsmouth) gig, we poured into the hotel bar and stayed up late, having the odd drink or two. Suddenly, at around 2.00 am, we all got really, really hungry - you know, that kind of hunger which makes you start dribbling just at the word 'food'. So we sent Stephen out with Melinda (choreographer) and a massive order for burgers, chips, chocolate - all the healthy stuff. Fantastic, just what I needed! I got to bed pretty late that night but was suddenly woken up by these voices outside my window. I jumped up, thinking it was a group of fans about to jump on me, until I heard this familiar sniggering and realised it was the guys trying to freak me out. I'll make sure I lock my windows from now on.
Shane, September 1995

The best thing in Boyzone, for me, is touring - that's the way I can give my time back to the fans. They're the people who are paying to see me and I want to give them the best show I can. If I see someone trying to catch my eye in the audience, I'll wave or blow them a kiss.
Stephen, July 1996

We clear everyone out, perform a ritual of stretching exercises and have a group chat. We don't talk about the show, we just chat about everyday stuff and catch up with each other, because we hardly see each other on our own during the day. Then I go and say a prayer on my own, ten minutes before I go onstage. I'm superstitious like that, and it gives me peace of mind.
Ronan, July 1996

Touring is great - the only problem I have is sleeping at night. I've never been able to sleep before 3.00 am, so I'm always in the bar until the early hours. But I love performing. I wait all day for those 90 minutes on stage. That's why we're here.
Mikey, July 1996

I love life on the road because I'm always the last one in the bar. I wish the others wouldn't go to bed so early, but I've learnt to enjoy my own company.
Keith, July 1996

It all goes so fast. You're on stage one minute, and the next you're saying, 'G'night!' It's mad. We get pelted with teddy bears - which we trip up on - knickers, bras, the usual.
  I'm in bed early every night. I can't handle drinking anymore! I was alright at the start of the tour, but now I can't get enough sleep because we work so hard.
Shane, July 1996

Birmingham was great because it was such a large arena and we had two nights back to back there. They were really fun shows, a lot of laughs! The crowds in Birmingham were brilliant - the atmosphere was electric! It was such a good feeling getting up on that stage - mind you, it's like that every night. That's not exclusive to Birmingham! It's not nerve-wracking playing arenas, really - you've got to get used to it, but it's nice to be at the stage where we can play arenas. I think we've coped with it well, considering it's our first arena tour. I don't know which song went down the best, though - the crowd were so good at Birmingham, they just went

mad for every song, so I couldn't say whether one of them was a particular favourite with them.
Ronan, August 1996

None of us slept the night before the first Wembley gig - we were all so nervous and hyped up! It's the place you always dream of playing - it's like, that's the most famous venue - you never think you'll be at the stage where you'll actually be able to play there. It was nice because loads of family and friends flew over from Dublin for it and they were dead proud. Mind you, we hardly got to see anyone we knew because there were so many other people there to speak to.

   We couldn't go out in London that weekend because we were all so shattered from all the excitement. All we could do was sleep - even Keith, who always usually goes out!

Shane, August 1996
The second leg of the tour started at the Glasgow SECC and it was funny because when we played the SECC on the last leg, it was the biggest venue and this time it was the smallest! That really made it sink in how far we'd come and what we'd achieved. I was relieved that we'd had a month's break in the middle of the tour because if we'd done two months solid of this tour, it would have killed us, I'm tellin' ya! I'm absolutely knackered now! I was glad we started the second half of the tour in Glasgow though, because they're a brilliant crowd. I've got a real soft spot for Scotland in general - the people really remind me of Dublin folk and you just know you're going to have a party when you're there.
Mikey, August 1996

We got a real buzz playing the arenas because we still don't consider ourselves pop stars - honest! Every crowd is different and the Manchester fans are really mad - it's a fantastic place to play. When I was onstage at the Nynex in front of about 15,000 people I remember thinking about the time we played in front of eight people in a hotel in Ireland - we still tried to give a good show then, as we always do.
Keith, August 1996

Cardiff was a brilliant show. It's a nice venue, that one - it's not one of the biggest venues, average size, but I really like it there. Should I be calling an arena average? I s'pose not! I loved seeing all the banners - I was really enjoying looking into the crowd and waving at people. After the gig we just went back to the hotel for a drink and a chat - we always have a talk about how the show went for each of us.
Stephen, August 1996

I've written material for our new album which will be out in a couple of months. Other than that - it's being on stage, I love that, but I think most of our fans know that! The feeling I'm giving the audience what they want and making them happy makes me really happy.
Stephen, September 1996

The last night of the tour killed me. I had to go to the studios. I couldn't even go to the party. I just needed to sleep, but I can't take time off - I can't afford to, this is too important. We're in the public eye. We had a lot of time to be with people at the start. We were all very happy and jolly lads when we started off, but then work kind of got on top of us and we're thinking about how we've got a lot more to do. Now we're all tired. We're still enjoying ourselves and having a laugh, but there's a lot more work and a lot more responsibility on our backs.
Ronan, November 1996

My drug is performing. When you stand on stage and look down on all the fans it's such a thrill. It's a real rush and a buzz.
Ronan, December 1996

I'm scared of losing my voice, particularly on stage. If I developed a serious problem with my voice, the whole tour would have been cancelled. The only way to deal with it is not to worry about it too much. Every singer fears getting nodules on their vocal cords. I don't even want to think about that!

The first show of each tour is scary because it's all new and changes are made up to the night before we start! We'll swap costumes around, change the choreography or the set, so we worry about wearing the wrong clothes or being in the wrong place. However, as soon as I walk out on stage the nervousness goes and everything clicks into place.
Ronan, June 1997

This is going to be our last tour for a while. We've done so much touring in the last three years we've decided it's time to do other things. After this tour we're going to take a break from touring for a while, hit you with something big and new.
Ronan, October 1997

The fans buy your singles, read the magazines you're in, listen to the radio stations you're on and watch all the television shows. Touring allows us to give something back. We try and give the best show we can.
Stephen, December 1997

This tour will be different because we'll be concentrating on the music a lot more this time. We'll be playing a lot of the new songs which are a bit slower so there won't be as much dancing around as there was in the past. We're not as fit as we used to be, we're old men now so I think we'll let the dancers do all the hard work this time round!
Ronan, October 1998

(Our worst gig was) probably the one at Docklands Arena in London about two and a half years ago - we only had two days to rehearse! The show was a bit ropey, and there was one acoustic song where it all fell apart. Ronan couldn't remember the words and we all drifted off stage in embarrassment.
Mikey, October 1998

Our five personalities come out. We're totally involved in putting our shows together from scratch. It's hard work, but it's worth it when you step out on stage with a show you're proud of. What is always important to us is that any new tour is better than the last. I love being on stage; I love performing.
Stephen, October 1998

We've cut a lot of old songs from our set. In the past I was so sick of singing those songs night after night that I used to change the lyrics. I'd make sure it sounded pretty similar to the original so that most people wouldn't notice but the others in the band certainly noticed, it would crack them up.
Ronan, October 1998

Every time I'm on stage I get a good feeling. A lot of the energy you get while performing is from the audience, and Boyzone's audiences are always brilliant.

I get more excited than nervous. We've been doing this for a long time now, so I'm kinda used to it. Sometimes I forget song lyrics or something, like last night I made a couple of mistakes, but you just have to laugh - it's not a major disaster or anything!
Stephen, December 1998

I've been listening to our album and trying to learn the words to the songs! The tour starts soon and I haven't got a clue what I'm singing. Honest to God, we've got this gig tomorrow night and I don't even know the lyrics to the song we're singing. I've had them faxed over today so that I get a chance to learn them in time.
Ronan

We haven't done a routine in ages, and I was rubbish at dancing even at the beginning. I don't care. I'm happy to make a show of meself and give people a laugh.
Keith, May 1999

We loved (our first Smash Hits tour). We were young and innocent and didn't know what we were getting ourselves into. We made friends with all the other bands, it was a magical time and we had a laugh.
Ronan, May 1999

(Yvonne and Jack) are at home now, but they've been on the road as much as possible - within reason, of course, 'cos Jack obviously can't travel too much. He was there on the whole UK tour and a bit of the European leg, but he wouldn't sleep on the bus so we always had to stay in hotels - he needs to get a good night's sleep!
Ronan, July 1999

The smaller venues are much more personal, we can see everybody when we play the smaller places. It's a big buzz to play venues like Wembley, but we still enjoy going back to the smaller places and being closer to our audience, closer to our fans.
Shane, 1999

Boyz Worldwide

I thought being a pop star would be so much more glamorous. When I was younger I imagined people like New Kids on the Block, Bros and Take That led a life of limos, flashy hotels and champagne.

I never expected to be so busy: Italy, Germany, Switzerland, Belgium, Britain then back to Ireland, and that's only one week!
Stephen, June 1995

We loved Glasgow. It's the place that most reminded us of home. We had a few hours to wander round the city and I spent the afternoon wandering round the shops, buying loads of clothes. Spent much too much money - bet that's hurt the bank balance! After the gig, we were in a serious partying mood and we ended up in the Tunnel Club. It was good, because everyone left us alone. We normally get hassle when we go to clubs and have to make a mad dash to the loo as soon as one of us gets spotted. This time, we only went to the loo when we wanted to!
Ronan, September 1995

I'm more mature and wise, but the main thing is I don't get homesick anymore. Well, not as much. I used to cry myself to sleep every night when I was away. This trip's been a doddle and it's the longest we've ever had.
Stephen, April 1996

It's tiring and it's good to get home. I've been most places now - a few times! We've been to Europe a lot, Thailand, Japan, we've been to Miami, Singapore and Hong Kong. The fans in the Far East are mad. They're crazy. They scream very loudly but they'll never run over and grab at us. They're very polite people and very soft. It's a whole different culture.
Stephen, September 1996

Australia is always great fun. The last time we went we shot our new video for 'Isn't It A Wonder' out there. We took a private plane to a place called Broken Hill and one of the engines went and we had to make an emergency landing. We were totally safe so it was a lot of fun, quite exciting. We landed at an airport in the desert. We swapped planes and flew on to do the video.
Ronan, March 1997

England is where we started and it's our second home. It's a place that has been very, very good to us.
Keith, March 1997

Indonesia is somewhere we're doing really well at the moment. We've gone six times platinum with our second album and we're going to go over and do a concert there at the end of the year.
Stephen, March 1997

Travelling can wind me up. If you have a lot of flights in one week it wears you out, it's sooo boring. You can't think straight or be sensible when things go wrong cos you're so tired and down. I find the best way to keep from getting angry is to sleep right through it all!
Keith, June 1997

Germany is very influenced by American music and culture so the Backstreet Boys are huge there. However, so is David Hasselhoff, so what does that say? Our fan base is growing there but we'd need to spend a lot more time out there to really make it big, and we don't have that time.
Shane, June 1997

I fell in love with Bahrain and Bali immediately. Then we went to India which was filled with beautiful buildings and people - but there was a lot of poverty and sickness too. We saw so many different things that most people just don't get to see.
Stephen, December 1997

I'm desperate to go to Africa, I've never been. It's the one place I want to visit.
Ronan, October 1998

I think Asia was one of the most amazing places, and Latin America, Argentina. It's a totally different culture there, it's a real experience. I love New York as well and I'm thinking of buying a place there one day.
Ronan

IRELAND
Views on the Emerald Isle

There are lots of British boy groups trying to be successful. When New Kids on the Block came along they hit right away because they were American. We're the first Irish pop group as most people associate Ireland with serious acts like U2, Sinead O'Connor and Enya.
Stephen, June 1995

It sounds funny but I find Irish people very different to English people. In Dublin, everyone told me to stop moaning and get on with it when I broke my leg. In England, I got loads of sympathy - everyone's more of a drama queen there. Not that I like to milk the sympathy, it's just that at home I have to remember to grin and bear it.
Shane, September 1995

Backstreet Boys

I do not agree whatsoever with what (the IRA) do. They're doing their own thing - I think it reflects badly on Irish people.
Shane, March 1996

I love Killarney, there are some lovely places over there. And Galway. And Dublin, of course, there's a good night life here. Belfast is nice too. There are loads of great places in Ireland!
Stephen, 1996

It's horrible to come from Ireland with the stuff that's going on. A lot of people in England are very ignorant about where the Troubles are. They don't realise that it is only in the north of Ireland, in six counties - there's 26 counties in the south where there isn't any trouble. Those people who call themselves the IRA are nothing to do with the Irish people. They're a gang of terrorists. A lot of people don't like us - I've been to a few nightclubs in Liverpool and Manchester and we've been turned away when they've heard our Irish accents.
Keith, March 1996

Last time I went home, it felt so good I kissed the ground when I walked off the plane!
Stephen, April 1997

As far as Irish people are concerned, if they see you in nice clothes and a good car they say you're showing off with your money. However, if you wear casual, normal clothes they turn round and say, 'Oh look, he's not doing well at all. I wear stuff like that,' and they diss you as a failure. I don't feel I'm showing off, it's just that I can now do what I want to do.
Shane, May 1997

I travel around the world and there's still nothing like coming back to Ireland. It's coming home to the food and the way of life there - I wouldn't give it up for anything. I'd rather go to Kerry on holiday than come down here to the Seychelles - I just love Ireland.
Ronan, December 1998

I don't think a president has the power that everybody thinks - they're just an ambassador for the country. But I could do a lot with Ireland, using my experiences of travelling round the world and seeing so many other countries.

Also, I like to be in touch with the people - I think that's very important - ah, it sounds like I'm doing a campaign here! I don't want to be anything special - I just want to be a normal person trying to relate to people.

If I do run for president, it'll be a long time away, but I'm honoured that people sometimes take me as an ambassador for the country. It's a very proud feeling for me. I don't see myself as a spokesman, but if they ask me I'll be there.

Would I talk about the Troubles in Ireland? Well, it's a sad and very difficult situation to talk about, but hopefully one day my children will live in a country that has peace. Please, God.
Ronan, January 1999

We're very Irish with our sense of humour. We're proud of being Irish, of our language and our accents. Our music has nothing to do with the traditional music, it's pop music. There's this rock tradition - Sinéad O'Connor, Therapy?, U2, Cranberries - but we were the first pop group and now there are loads, which I think we opened the door for. Irish people are great at entertaining and parties, but if you're successful and you're from the place, they think they own you, which can be tough. You get slagged just walking down the street.
Stephen, March 1999

I get quite a bit of hassle in Ireland. The Irish can be quite hard on their own and I get a fair bit of abuse. I've had death threats and stuff like that but I don't let it bother me. Most people have accepted us but I've been beaten up in a club, that kind of thing.

What people forget is that I'm the same person I was years ago. I'm just lucky enough to have enough money in my pocket to have a good time. But I think people like us because we are very well-mannered - we've got the best manners in pop.
Keith, May 1999

We are as big in Northern Ireland as we are in the Republic and we are helping to bridge the gap. We want to do our bit for peace but I'm not sure we would ever make a political statement in our music. We just write pop music to make people happy and make kids smile.

We aren't a controversial band and we don't particularly want to be. We have a nice guy image but we've all got big hearts.
Stephen, May 1999

The greatest place in the world is Dublin of course. There's nothing like travelling the world but it's always great to come home. Saying that, Bali comes a pretty close second!
Keith, June 1999

AMERICA
Their struggle to break big Stateside

It is the biggest market in the world and probably the hardest to crack. We'd need to spend such a long time there and so we decided to approach it in a different way by making it in Latin America first and letting our success filter through.
Stephen, June 1997

It's a country I've wanted to visit for ages. I think every band looks to North America as another step in their career so, yeah, it's very important for Boyzone because if America accepts us then I think the whole world will accept us even more.

I've got a good feeling about this… yes, I've got a really good feeling about this, I have to say. It's been building up since we came over, with the fans and all the Hard Rock Cafe parties we've been doing. Basically the Hard Rock have taken us on and let us have an album launch party in every major city in the US for press, media and competition winners. They've been cool!
Ronan, October 1997

Being in the States has made us all very ambitious again. When we started out in Ireland and in the UK we made mistakes. Now we know so much more - we know how to talk to people, we know what people can see and what we can do behind closed doors!
Keith, October 1997

America's not the sort of place we expect to get noticed when we're here, I don't think anyone does! I think even U2 could walk down the road and not get noticed. They can do that in Dublin as well but it's kind of different for them because their fans are much older.
Ronan, October 1997

U2

A lot of Americans are comparing us to The Beatles, which is a great honour! One difference they haven't picked up on is that The Beatles were English and we're Irish, so we're probably more like U2. At the end of the day, hopefully people will just take us for what we are.
Shane, October 1997

The Spice Girls' success has been phenomenal and they've definitely opened the door to America, which used to be completely R&B, but now it's more open to pop groups. So hopefully things will work out for us here too.
Keith, October 1997

Breaking America is still something that interests us but if it happens, it happens. We're not going to worry about it cos it's such a tough market to break. I've got my TV presenting stuff still to come as well, that's still happening. That should be great but it's not going to detract from the music, that'll come first for me every time. I'll probably do that after the tour finishes in November, it's the only chance I'll get.
Ronan, October 1998

I think we're going to go over there and let people know what we've done and achieved in other countries, so we won't have to start at the very beginning again. It's good timing for us as the pop market's really opened up over there, what with The Spice Girls, Backstreet Boys and 'N Sync.
Stephen, April 1999

We're going over to do the Rosie O'Donnell Show, which we're looking forward to, but we made the decision not to really do (promotion) - it'll be six months of our lives to promote over there and we're not prepared to sacrifice that. Maybe after we've had a break we'll think differently.
Ronan, June 1999

We're tired, but life has never been better. We're off to LA tomorrow actually. It's funny, everybody's thinking that Boyzone are breaking up and in fact we're going to break America.
Ronan, August 1999

We're off to LA to do a turn in General Hospital which is a big American soap opera. We're going to be performing as ourselves in the local nightclub. I've never actually seen the show before, but I'm sure it will be good.
Ronan, August 1999

We've signed over in the States and we've been over a few times for promotional trips. They've taken on 'No Matter What', which is doing really well over there. We're very optimistic about how things might take off over there, and we're looking forward to going back. It's a country we haven't been to as many times as other territories but hopefully we'll be back there soon.
Stephen, 1999

Loves and losses
Loves relationships, marriages, kids

I'm nearly at the end of my tether. I'm going to have security posted at every door for the birth. No-one is coming near. I just don't know why the press can't leave us in peace to have the baby.
Mikey, 1996

It's been hard doing these rehearsals because I keep thinking, 'Am I a daddy yet?' I haven't got a mobile phone, but the others have all got them and they'll be rung up when it's time for me to go to the hospital - I want to be there for the birth. The trouble is, every time someone's phone rings, I think it's for me. It could be difficult if the baby isn't born for another week, because I'll probably have to miss a few of the early dates.
Keith, 1996

The media went mad. When Lisa got pregnant, she was on the front cover of every paper in Ireland. And that's how everyone found out, I didn't tell many people because I didn't think it was anyone else's business. But I'm happy now - I wouldn't change a thing.
Keith, April 1996

I'm more focused. Now I've got a little person depending on me, I'm not as mixed up as I was. There was a time when I was uncomfortable because I wanted to be making harder music. I was confused, mixed-up and edgy. Now I don't mind any more. I'm doing what I'm doing for her; before I was doing it for myself.
Mikey, June 1996

We had talked quite a lot about having children. With me being away so much, we thought it was a good idea for Lisa to have a part of me all the time. We had yet to come to a final decision, but God made it for us and we are delighted.

At the moment, I am putting everything into my work because I want to secure my future. My schedule for the next year is fully booked, so as soon as I get enough time to marry the girl, I'll do it. I want it to be social, a huge white wedding with six bridesmaids, so I want to be able to prepare it properly.

Keith, July 1996

that, because they do not have the maternal instincts women do. Now that I'm a father, I really pine for her when I'm away.

She's my precious little angel and I speak to her on the phone every day - even though she can't talk!

Mikey, July 1996

I knew I'd have to do photos of the baby with somebody or I'd be looking over my shoulder all the time for the paparazzi, y'know? So we decided to do photos with *Hello* and get it over with. At the end of the day, it's a classy magazine, the interview had everything I wanted to say and it was better than doing

Keith with Lisa and baby Jordan

In all the madness, my daughter is the only sane thing I have and I'm madly in love with her, although I wasn't sure I would be before she was born. I think all men feel like

the tabloids. It wasn't about money - in fact, the tabloids offered twice as much. But I wanted the best for my little babby, y'know?

Keith, August 1996

Marriage is a bond between a man and a woman for life. To share the good times and the bad, the joy, the happiness and even the loneliness. That's what I want from marriage - to share the rest of my life with someone who loves me and I love the same.
Mikey, November 1996

for? It's not like we don't love each other,' I said. 'We've been planning on getting married, we've been planning on getting a house together, we'll just be doing it a bit earlier.' Lisa was grand after that.
Keith, November 1996

Ronan with Yvonne

I was sitting in the *Top Of The Pops* dressing room waiting to perform 'Father And Son' when I found out my girlfriend Lisa was three months pregnant. I was very upset and scared. I went home the next day and took Lisa to the clinic, but she had to go in on her own. I waited in the car, otherwise the press would have known straight away. When Lisa came out crying I knew for sure she was pregnant. I convinced myself I was strong. I had to be. I asked Lisa, 'What are you getting upset

By the time Jordan was born I had been through every emotion there is. I'm only 21 and I felt as though I was 40. I'd always been very happy-go-lucky with no responsibilities and all of a sudden I had someone who was relying on me 100 per cent. It made me think a lot. It made me grow up.
Keith, November 1996

We had talked about getting married in June. But when we were on the golf course (in the Caribbean) we thought it was such a perfect place and we suddenly said, 'Why wait?'
Ronan, May 1998

(Yvonne and I) first met when we were 13 or 14, but we lost contact for years, and then when we met up again we were best friends for a year and a half. But it got to the point where I either had to tell her that I loved her or walk away and never see her again. Luckily, I chose the first option because I knew in my heart it was right.
Ronan, August 1998

I take Jordan round the supermarket and we always get stuck at the pick'n'mix counter for hours, eating half the shop! We don't cook, and our food comes from M&S. We have our own weird fantasies that we'd never tell anyone about so we have to go and buy everything ourselves.
Keith, September 1998

I decided to tell people about Lisa when she became pregnant, because it was important to me that I shouldn't be seen to be denying the mother of my child. It was important for her.
Keith, September 1998

My mum and dad knew (about our wedding) cos they had to look after Jordan when we went to Las Vegas. My best mates at home knew. Ronan and Stephen had to be told or they wouldn't have been there, then we told Mikey and Shane. The first people we told after the wedding were Lisa's parents and her friends. We'd had a few celebratory drinks by that point so we phoned everyone. No phone bill spared!
Keith, September 1998

I love my family, simply because they're my family. May family are incredibly, incredibly close. And, of course, I love my closest friends in the world as well, because they mean so much to me.
Ronan, October 1998

The only thing that scares me is the fear of something happening to my family. I worry that they might not be there when I get home. There have been a few times when I've rung home and no-one has answered and I've had a panic attack. But, thank God, there's never been anything wrong.
Keith, October 1998

(Married life is) amazing. It's everything I wanted it to be and Yvonne is an incredible woman. Whenever I see her, my tummy turns upside down and my head goes light. It's incredible!
Ronan, October 1998

The only difference once you're married is that life's not about just you any more, it's about you and your wife together. You put her feelings before your own.
Shane, October 1998

The birth of your first child, it's the biggest thing to happen in anyone's life. Hopefully it won't be the last either.
  I wouldn't miss the birth for the world! I'll be there. I'm hoping to go to the pre-natal classes and all that stuff. Unfortunately I'll probably be on tour for a lot of that but I'll go whenever I can.
Ronan, October 1998

I joined Boyzone when I was 16, and I've travelled around the world three or four times, meeting loads of different people. I feel like I've done what a lot of other people don't do until they're 30 or 40 years of age. The next step for me was to marry the woman I love and wanted to spend the rest of my life with.
Ronan, December 1998

the difference between right and wrong. Whether they'll take any notice of what I say is a different story!
Ronan, January 1999

I speak to Yvonne maybe ten times a day. We just phone to let each other know how our day's going. I think it's very important to communicate. I think

Becoming a father is scary and daunting, but I'm looking forward to it, I have to say. I'm reading all the books and I'm trying to learn as best I can, but I'll do what I can when I get there. I just wanna take it as it comes, not think about it too much.

I'm a very strict person, I think, and I'll be strict with my child. Moral values are very important to me and I hope I'll teach my child

understanding is very important as well. Caring, loving - that's what makes a good husband.

We both work hard and we'll continue to do so in the future - I don't believe in the man being the breadwinner or anything like that. I do hog the remote control, though. When it comes to technical things in the house, leave it to me.
Ronan, January 1999

I'm a lot younger than my parents were when they had me, so I'm going to try to relate to my kids a lot better. Not that I didn't relate to my parents - it's just that I want to be young and be able to go down to the pub and enjoy a pint with my child. I want to grow up with them - play football and stuff, you know? I'll change the nappies and everything. Whatever it takes.
Ronan, January 1999

I wouldn't give anybody advice about being a father. It's just something you have to adjust to. (Ronan) will have to know how to change a nappy straightaway. He'll be thrown in at the deep end, but he's a sensible lad and he doesn't need anybody telling him what to do.
Keith, March 1999

The boys are nearly as excited as I am about the baby. They see it as an extension of the Boyzone family! Keet's son Jordan and Mikey's daughter Hannah are at the ('You Needed Me') video shoot and I play with them when there's a spare moment. I need the practice!
Ronan, March 1999

Ronan will probably find it tougher than he imagines. It will be great excitement when the child is born, but once the child is born and it's just him, Yvonne and the baby there, and all the relatives have gone home, you have to deal with it. I didn't get any sleep for ages, and then I had to go straight out on tour. I was pretty wrecked! It was a really crazy time.
Mikey, March 1999

We definitely won't be starting a family at the moment. Maybe in about five years' time, but Easther's going to be getting her career back on the road in the next six months with Eternal. I don't believe in the man being the only breadwinner, so there are no plans at the moment.
Shane, March 1999

I am seeing Karen Corradi (dancer) and she's the loveliest women I've ever met. We have a lot of fun together and we're great friends. Our relationship started off on a mates basis and then we got together properly at the end of the tour.
Mikey, April 1999

I worry about Jack every minute of the day. I'm a nervous wreck and if I hear a little cough or a little cry then I go running in to check on him. The reality is, though, that he just needs his nappy changing or feeding or something like that. Fatherhood is absolutely brilliant. Jack is on tour with me because it is very important for him to grow up around me.

I don't want to be an absent father. I don't want him to grow up and us grow apart. My life has changed so much being a husband and being a father. Having a little bundle in my hands has put my life into perspective. There is absolutely no question that I would give it all up for him.

He's got a little smile now and every day there's something different - something new to look at. I wouldn't want to miss that. Imagine how I'd feel if I came back off tour and he was a different person. I just hope I'm a good dad. I suppose I'll have to ask him in 20 years.
Ronan, May 1999

(Being a dad) is grand and he's healthy and strong - no problem. My life's changed a lot, but it's been fantastic. A lot of things come into perspective when you have a child.
Ronan, June 1999

Fatherhood is great. My lad Jack is four months old now and huge. He weighs the same as an 18 month old I picked up the other day. We'll have to cut down on the Farley's Rusks or maybe it's that Jack has Guinness flowing through his veins - like his dad!
Ronan, July 1999

(Yvonne) is a down-to-earth, grounded person. My mother was head of the house, and I wanted a strong woman. Yvonne is full of strength.

It's her choice to give up modelling. She wants to be there for the children, to raise our family. We are talking about a second baby, and we'll go from there. I'd like to have quite a few. We've got a big house with six bedrooms and we intend to fill it.
Ronan, July 1999

My son will be brought up just as my mother raised me. I won't be strict as long as he respects what I have to say and listens to me. I am rather worried about sex education, but we'll cross that bridge when we come to it. My parents weren't open about sex at all, and I was a late starter. I had some rather silly ideas when I was a boy. I thought that if you kissed you could get a girl pregnant. I will be open with Jack, but I will tell him that chastity is important.
Ronan, July 1999

(Mikey and Keith's children) travel with us as much as possible as well. But it can be hard for them and it's hard for us, too - we're working all the time and it can get frustrating when you can't give them the time you want. But they love Jack, especially Jordan. He sees him the most, I guess - he spends loads of time with him and he's great with him.
Ronan, July 1999

Life at home is magic. I don't get home enough but when I do I make the most of it. At the moment the weather is good so we're having barbecues and stuff like that. Jack's growing up and we're laughing every day. Life's good, never been better.
Ronan, August 1999

It can be really difficult being away from Yvonne and Jack when we're on the road, but a lot of the time they do come out and travel with us. Us lads are very lucky to have three happy, healthy children in the band. I want to take Jack around the world and show him lots of different cultures.
Ronan, August 1999

Losses: The death of Ronan's mum

I have been walking around like a zombie. There is a massive gap in my life, a huge void.
Ronan, February 1998

My mother was such a central point of my life, a foundation. To lose her was devastating but (wife) Yvonne has kept me going. She hasn't taken Mam's place but I get the same feeling of strength from her.
Ronan, May 1998

My mam was everything to me, but my dad was never very emotional. He never showed us much love. There has always been a distance between me and my dad.
Ronan, November 1998

There has always been a distance between me and my dad. My mam was everything to me, but my dad was never very emotional. He never showed us much love.
Ronan, November 1998

I've changed so much over this last year. So much that I couldn't even begin to put it into words. I'll never be the same person I was before my mother's death. It was the most painful experience of my life. In some ways it's still with me. There isn't a day goes by that I don't miss her. And it's changed

my attitude to life. Now I won't put off until tomorrow what I can do today. Because you never know.
Ronan, January 1999

My mother's death was the most painful thing, because I was so close to her. I think when you lose someone so dear it really encourages you to seize every day, you know, because no one knows how long they've got.
Ronan, February 1999

I'll never get over my mum's death. I've just tried to keep going. It's harder now. When I look at Jack I can't accept the fact that my mother has never seen him.
  I look into his eyes and into my wife's eyes and realise that my mum wasn't there to witness the two most important events of my life - getting married and having a baby - and that really hurts. My mother was an exceptional human being and she would have loved nothing more than seeing my first child being born. She adored kids and they adored her too. I look at Jack and I see some of her in him and it makes me tearful. It's so unfair that she did not see him.
Ronan, May 1999

I learn to deal with (Mum's death) every day, that's life. I am very busy and my marriage and the arrival of my son Jack has helped. but it still hasn't hit me yet that she's really gone. I still think that she's just away on holiday. When the phone rings I think it might be her.
Ronan, July 1999

Stevo's Statement

How the first gay boyband member came out - and the diplomatic answers to leading questions before he did

Before...

Everyone used to fancy Wonder Woman, I know I did.
Stephen, December 1995

When the right person comes along, I'll know and then I'll do something about it. But until then, I'm working really hard. We all are. It's hard for the lads, having kids and being away. I'd hate that. I have become an uncle, though. My sister had a boy, Jordan, and my sister-in-law gave birth to a son, Brandon, two weeks earlier. So what with Mikey and Keith's babies as well, it's like I'm an uncle four times over! I've got enough kids to look after, thanks!
Stephen, July 1996

I suppose (In ten years' time) I'll be the same. Except older. Much older. I'll be married with children - aww, a couple of lickle children.
Stephen, September 1996

I think the Spice Girls would be fun (to snog under the mistletoe). We've bumped into them several times now and they're brilliant. Which Spice Girl in particular? Now, that would be telling! Let's just say I'd like to have all of them under the mistletoe kissing me!
Stephen, December 1996

I know many girls around the world, but let's just say I'm not getting married in the morning! I don't miss having a relationship - there'll be plenty of time for that.
Stephen, July 1997

Stephen with Emma 'Baby Spice' Bunton

I don't think you can ever find true happiness. You can be content, but happiness changes. You can be happy one day and sad and tortured the next day, and that's not really anything to do with outside things, that's to do with how you feel inside.
Stephen

I've been romantically linked with Baby Spice, all the Eternal girls and Zo' Ball and I wish I could see them all of the time 'cause they are really good friends of mine. They're all in the same business, so they understand the hassles. If you're not in this business, it's hard to understand the here-today-gone-tomorrow lifestyle.
Stephen, October 1997

So I'm not getting married in the morning - that doesn't mean I'm frustrated. I've got too many people around me, too hectic a schedule. I never feel lonely - I'm too busy to be lonely.
Stephen, October 1998
Everyone keeps asking me when it's gonna be my turn so, in a way, I do feel as if I'm under more pressure to get married. But I'm only 22 and there's plenty of time to settle down.
Stephen, October 1998

I really like natural-looking girls with naturally curly brown hair and brown eyes. I don't like her to be taller than me. I like outgoing, cheerful, happy girls.
Stephen, March 1999

I'm just not ready (to settle down). I look at the other guys and see how hard it is to keep a relationship going. Shane hasn't seen Easther for a month and a half, and that must be really hard. I'm not ready to deal with that now. I'm enjoying life. I'm doing what I want to do - going out shopping, taking care of myself and looking after my family. At the moment, I'm concentrating on my career. I know a lot of people, But I'm not getting married tomorrow, you know what I mean? When I meet the right person, maybe in a few years, then I'll settle down
Stephen, April 1999

I find it easier to trust people within the business because they understand what you're going through. For instance yesterday, I was talking to Geri Halliwell and she's lovely. I also know Shaznay from All Saints quite well. But I've always been a bit of a loner and I like to have time to myself to watch TV and lie in the bath.
Stephen, May 1999

All Saints

After...

This is the most important day of my life. From today I will have the freedom to finally be myself.
I wanted my fans to hear the facts from me before anyone else got the chance to publish a twisted version of the truth.
Stephen, June 1999

I think the time has come to be honest and tell everyone that I am gay. I owe it to all Boyzone fans to know the truth.
'm not ashamed of coming out like this, my family and close friends have known for a long time. My family have been so supportive and they are here for me now.
I want my fans to know that I haven't changed, I'm still the same Steve and I hope they will all understand and support me.
Stephen, June 1999

Talking about this takes courage and I'll always love him for that. He and (boyfriend) Eloy make each other really happy and nothing should stand in the way of happiness.
Ronan, June 1999

We're all very proud of him. I'm glad Steve has decided to do this. This is about his happiness and being able to live his life with honesty and pride. It changes nothing between us.
Mikey, June 1999

Not once in the last six years, have I been able to relax and be myself. I have never, ever denied being gay. I don't know how many times I've used the phrase, 'I'll settle down when the right person comes along,' And now that Ronan and the boys have started families, it has become harder to explain.
Stephen, June 1999

The fans stood by me when Yvonne and I got married and I hope they stand by Stephen.
Ronan, June 1999

It's Stephen's business who he goes out with. I love him like a brother.
Keith, June 1999

In this day and age, it is no big deal to be gay. There is no problem here. In fact, we are really happy Steve has decided to make this step.
Shane, June 1999

I knew he was gay for years. A lot of my friends are gay and

Stephen with
Cerys Matthews,
Rik Mayall and
Jane Horrocks

I don't like the Church turning away from people because of their sexuality. I am glad it's not so difficult to be gay in Ireland now.
Ronan, July 1999

Stephen is like a changed man since coming out and admitting he's gay. He is so much more relaxed and can just be himself and live his own life.

We get loads of gay rainbow flags at our gigs now, it's unreal. We never got that before and I don't think it was ever cool for gay people to come to our shows, but now they seem to love it.
Ronan, July 1999

(Coming out) was Stephen's decision and we all admire him for it. It was a big move and it was tough, but given the response of the fans I think it was definitely a positive one. You know when Yvonne and myself decided to get married we were scared about how the fans would react and they've been fantastic.
Ronan, August 1999

Battle Of The Boybands
Their views on rivals - Five, etc - and vice versa

There has never been any animosity between us (and Take That), but obviously we're going get compared to them. When I met Robbie recently he was such a nice guy and he gave us all some great advice - 'Keep your head and don't forget who you are or where you're from'. That's just so true and that's exactly what they've all managed to do.
Ronan, January 1995

We saw (Take That) on the Brits show and they were good. Really good. In fact we're poohing our pants because their song ('Back For Good') is so good.
Ronan, March 1995

A newspaper recently had something in about us putting Take That down, and it really upset us. We've never said anything bad about them. We really admire them.
Keith, March 1995

We've been called the Irish Take That, but that's stupid. If there had been four of us we'd have been the Irish Bad Boys Inc; with three we'd be the Irish EYC. It's ridiculous.
Keith, June 1995

We've been called the Irish Take That from day one and we don't mind. We don't blame people because there are five of them and five of us. They were labelled the new New Kids when they started and it hasn't done them any harm. Hopefully we'll soon develop our own style so we won't be in their shadow forever.
Mikey, June 1995

I don't think we'd swap places with (Take That), because we don't have the experience to handle what they're going through. I don't think they've got much of a life any longer. If you want to be in a famous pop group and have Number 1s, then you have to be prepared to put your life on hold for a few years. We're just not that ready yet.
Ronan, June 1995

I really respect Take That but I think they should have done a concert at Wembley Stadium with Robbie to say farewell. All they did was a press conference and I just thought, 'Come on, lads, give us a bit more!' It was a flat way to end.
Ronan, March 1996

I am really looking forward to being respected some day. Take That did it, they had respect from the industry. I suppose it may take a while for Boyzone, but I feel we're making steps in the right direction. I suppose it's what every singer and songwriter wants, at the end of the day.
Ronan, July 1996

Five

We're not into the Take That sort of show. We do our own thing and nobody tells us how we should behave.
Ronan, May 1997

I think (Five) are very good. I just think they should concentrate more on their music and not on being hard men! Maybe we had an attitude problem when we were just starting, but I don't think so - we were never ones to slate other bands.
Keith, October 1998

Everyone knows the pop industry is very fickle. People forget easily. Look at Take That, people have forgotten them already, I can't understand why. Take That were a great band.
Ronan

I think (Five) are very nice guys and I get on with them well. I think some people take them the wrong way, but I think they're cool. When they first came out, I think they were so paranoid about people having a go at them that they put on a front. But it's fine now - we chat and stuff.
Keith, January 1999

You can tell us we're The Bee Gees if you like - as long as I get to be Barry - but there's no point in kidding ourselves, the perception of us won't change. I saw A1 supporting Steps and they looked really inexperienced, and I remember what that feels like. You think you know what you're doing but really you haven't a clue.
Shane, May 1999

Me and Scott were on TV with Keith and Mikey having a laugh. They were both saying 'Don't buy Five's album!' and we were saying 'Boyzone are rubbish!'
Rich Five, May 1999

You Gotta Have Faith
Boyzone on their religious beliefs

I don't know what form (life after death) would take. It's a spiritual thing. I believe in a heaven and a hell, but not like the accepted view of what they look like. And I believe you'll be categorised in that world by what you're like in this world - by your intentions and your points of view.
Mikey, February 1996

Who knows where spirits may end up. I believe because I'd be afraid that if I didn't they'd come and haunt me to prove it. Have I seen any? God has never wanted me to see one so I haven't, so far.
Ronan

My mum wanted me to be a priest.
Stephen, May 1996

I've had lots of spiritual experiences. I can't really describe it except to say that a spirit or a ghost has touched me. In fact I'm in contact with a spirit quite regularly.
Shane

I've never lost my way so much that I've felt I've had to pray for guidance as to what to do next. At least I never used to, now I'm not so sure, heh heh! Basically, I believe everything is mapped out for us. God knows what is going to happen and it all happens for a reason.

You think about death and you can't understand it. Right now I can say that's the way things happen, but if someone close to me died then, yes, I would wonder why it had happened. But I believe when you're meant to go, then you are meant to go. It's a very sad thing but you go on to a better place. I definitely believe we go on to a better place.

My nan died when I was younger. I remember it very clearly. I was very close to her and it broke my heart at the time. I have only one grandparent left and that's all. But it didn't make me question God or his reasoning. These things are just meant to happen.
Ronan

I believe in something after death but I don't know what it is. I mean, there must be something afterwards and I hope I get there. So I do believe in it. I do, I do, I do!
Stephen, September 1996

I'm a religious person and I believe God has set out a path for me and that is the road I am taking. Yes, I have lost the innocence of the child I was at 16 but then I've seen more countries and met more people in the last three years than most people do in a whole lifetime! The experience has opened our minds to the world. It's fantastic!
Ronan, January 1997

Everybody is made to be the way God intended. I wouldn't want to be anybody else because I'm so lucky.
Ronan, January 1997

I don't go to Mass as much as I'd like. I haven't had the chance. I pray to God. I think everybody who's in trouble must pray to God at some time. I love going to church.
Stephen, July 1996

At home, I see people of 17 walking down the street with babies in prams, when they aren't mentally or physically prepared to be parents. I will sleep with someone only when I'm ready to be a father, because that's what my religion says.
Ronan, May 1997

I have always been a true believer in God and I do try to follow my religion, although I don't agree with the Church's stance on divorce.
  I often talk to God at night and before a concert, and I would love to say I go to Mass every Sunday, but it wouldn't be true and my mother taught me never to tell a lie.

If I did, she always knew and she'd belt me across the backside. I'd never do anything to cross her, because she gave me everything.
Ronan, May 1997

A one-night stand isn't something that interests me at all. To me, sex is something you save for marriage, for that one person you will spend the rest of your life with.

Call me idealistic, but I know it's achievable. If you love somebody then anything is possible and, because I come from a Catholic family, I've been raised to respect sex.
Ronan, September 1997

I usually try to go to Midnight Mass 'cause there aren't as many children there - even if I'm on my knees praying or whatever, they'll still come up and ask for an autograph.
Stephen, January 1998

Everyone has different ideas about the Catholic religion. Me mam for example gave up meat on a Friday. I have my own beliefs. I believe in the Bible but I don't do everything that the Church tells me to, for example I don't agree with everything it says about divorce. I don't believe people can tell you there's a right way or a wrong way. Only God can tell me that.
Ronan

My mam doesn't agree with Mass on Christmas Eve so we all go on Christmas Day, the day of the Lord, to see my mother and father sing in the church choir.
Keith, January 1998

(Faith)'s important to me; it keeps me going. I'm a Catholic, but I don't believe all the teachings of the Church - they're not appropriate for this day and age. I believe in the Bible and God, and that's as far as I'll go.
Ronan, February 1999

I started reading books because I was getting so down. I'd have to be all happy in interviews and then I'd get home and realise, 'God, I'm so empty. Where am I in life? Where am I going?' So I started reading a lot of spiritual books. I read

The Game Of Life and *Conversations With God* and it was brilliant. I also have acupuncture which relieves stress. I get eight needles stuck in every month or so, and they put little clamps on the end which make the needles more potent. It rejuvenates you by unblocking your energy blocks, so you don't feel so stressed-out.
Stephen, May 1999

The Church is so corrupt. Every time you open the paper you read something about a priest who has been up to something. It's sickening.

I'd like to say more, but I don't push my ideas onto anyone. It's okay for Bono to give his views, but it's not the same for someone from Boyzone to do it. Our fans are so young, and so are we. I hope that we have been morally good for our fans. We are not like Oasis, we don't throw TVs about. We are careful what we do and say. We know we have such an influence.
Ronan, July 1999

George Michael

Keatings Quest
The first solo group member on his aims and ambitions

No, I wouldn't like to be a solo artist, not right now anyway. Everyone seems to see me as the Gary Barlow of the band but I don't see it that way. I do what I do and have a laugh and look forward to a future with Boyzone. It's nice to be able to share things with other people - it must be lonely on the road if you're on your own. Solo artists tend to go into themselves a lot.
Ronan

We do talk about (having a normal job) sometimes. I say, 'Oh I wish I had a nine-to-five job', but we would never have our lifestyle or house if it wasn't for this job. As much as I say, 'God, I'd love to be at home', I'd probably be climbing the walls with boredom after three weeks. I wouldn't be able to survive now without the music industry. Besides, Yvonne never asks me to do anything different.
Ronan, September 1998

It's not as though Boyzone are splitting up; George Michael released 'Careless Whisper' when he was still in Wham!. But eventually, if the band doesn't last forever, I want to still be doing this.
Ronan, March 1999

It's a bit strange doing a single on my own ('When You Say Nothing At All') but it's been a lot of fun. I'm really looking forward to it coming out.
Ronan, April 1999

I have to say I can't wait to become a solo artist. Boyzone aren't going to split up tomorrow, but we talk about it. I have wanted to go solo for a long time. I want to do songs with people like George Michael and R Kelly. If the lads were upset about me leaving, I'd hate to think that we'd fall out, but I don't want to go down with a sinking ship. I want to go out when we're at the top.
Ronan, May 1999

It's something I have wanted to do for a long time, even before I was in the band. I don't know what's round the corner. The split won't be tomorrow but I don't think it'll be a million miles away.
Ronan, May 1999

It wasn't until the people from the movie (*Notting Hill*) approached me and I jumped at the opportunity. I thought it was brilliant, and they gave me the song 'cos that thought I was the right person to do it - which was great! It had definitely been on the cards for all of us to pursue individual careers in music, and it was the perfect time for me to do it. Hopefully I'll launch a solo album in late March next year off the back of it - if everything goes to plan. I'll start writing the album in September out in America, then finish it off when I get back to the UK. I'm really looking forward to it - I've got loads of ideas already.
Ronan, July 1999

Going solo at the Fleadh festival in London recently was nerve-racking - a baptism of fire that took my back to my early days with the band. I'll do more solo gigs next year and I'll probably include Boyzone songs like 'No Matter What'.
Ronan, July 1999

I find I'm always looking behind me when I'm doing TV shows - I forget they're not there, and it's like, 'Arrrggh, I'm on my own up here!' But I guess I'll get used to it eventually.
Ronan, July 1999

Everyone around me seems confident 'When You Say Nothing At All' is going to be Number 1, but I'm really nervous about it. It shifted 35,000 copies in the first two days. If it does make Number 1 it'll be weird being there without the rest of the boys.
And even then I'll be hoping I'm knocked off again after two weeks. That's when Westlife release their new track 'If I Let You Go' - and as their co-manager I'd happily be beaten by them.
Ronan, July 1999

It's a daunting time for me. It's all new, it's gonna be scary being away from the lads but it's something I want to do and I'm looking forward to it.
Ronan, August 1999

It's understandable that people are saying (a solo career might signal the end of Boyzone), but we don't want to break up, this is something we want to do as individuals.
Ronan, August 1999

The song ('When You Say Nothing At All') is beautiful - it was the film company who chose it and asked me to record it, but I don't think I could have chosen better, it's a fabulous track. I've seen the movie a couple of times now and I love it - it has some really funny moments. 'When You Say' appears at a really beautiful and important moment in the film, and people keep telling me how much they remember the song after the film is finished because of that.
It's a really proud feeling. I'm really nervous about how it's going to go, but I'm also very, very excited. The day I arrived at the set to shoot the video, it suddenly hit me that I was going to be there alone - not surrounded by the other four boys, and that was a bit strange at first, but a big buzz. It's a new chapter, and I can't wait to see what happens.
Ronan, August 1999

I was so lucky being asked 'When You Say Nothing At All' for the movie Notting Hill. It's brilliant being able to pursue a solo career and still be in Boyzone - not many people in bands get that opportunity!
Ronan, August 1999

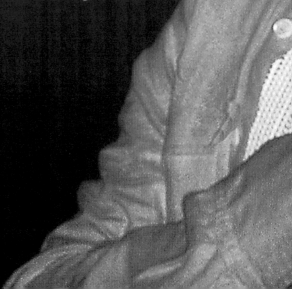

I went to the (*Notting Hill*) premiere and (Julia Roberts) came over to me and said that she thought that my song was her favourite from the movie! I was very happy about that, as you can imagine.
Ronan, August 1999

I'm on top of the world - it's so great to see the fans like my solo work. I'll celebrate till late but I've got to get up early to fly to LA to work on my solo album.
Ronan, August 1999

Solo Album
I'm going to be writing songs with Barry Gibb from The Bee Gees. We're flying out to America for three weeks on Monday to write for my solo album which should be out in March.
Ronan, July 1999

Ronan with Julia Roberts

Barry Gibb

Boyz On Boyz
Views on themselves, each other and relationships between them

I used to look after the lads all the time. I'd ring and check they knew what time they had to be up and this was when I was 16! It's just progressed from there. Now, I don't have to look after them in that way, partly because we have people doing it for us. However, I try to look after Stephen as much as I can. Because he's such an open person he can get hurt very easily and that's dangerous in the music industry. But Steve's a good judge of character and he can tell the good from the bad. I see him as my little brother really. As for the others, the boys will always call me and ask me what's happening but I don't look after them anymore, so to speak.
Ronan

Stephen's okay to share with, but he does have his moods. I could never share a room with Mikey and Keith, though. They usually share with each other, but at times they can't even cope with being in the same room together!
Shane, September 1995

I'm very, very close to Ronan and Shane. I'm close to them all, but more so to Ronan and Shane. Sometimes it changes. On this trip, me and Keith have spent a lot of time together. We both can't sleep, so he comes into my room and we'll talk, then go to the gym or something.

When the band started, I went really into myself. I stayed in another building to the rest of them because I didn't want to upset them. I didn't talk much, got very depressed, I just wanted to be at home. But I won't go like that again.

I get frightened a lot. I'm scared of getting hurt. I don't want this job to hurt me in years to come. I'm happy and I'd like to enjoy it. I'd like people to let me enjoy it. I'm really soft. I mean, I could cry talking about things.
Stephen, April 1996

Myself and Mikey get on great, but if we share a room we end up killing each other. We've tried it a few times, but he snores and he's got smelly feet. I'm sure he has a few things to say about me too!

Stephen likes being on his own. Stephen's very shy, very quiet, very secretive. He doesn't like anyone knowing his business. At first it was weird, but we respect that about him now. We used to slag him off for being pretentious, but we soon realised it was just him being friendly.
Keith, April 1996

Mikey and Keith have a tendency to sit on their arses too much when it comes to practising their dance steps, and Stephen's not a lot better. It's up to me to crack the whip a little!
Shane, 1996

73

I never wished I was anybody else, I'm happy with who I am. But it would be interesting to be the Pope for a day. Everybody looks up to him and everything he says is right, you know. I'm not sure I could handle kissing all that tarmac though!
Ronan

I respect Ronan for not drinking because of his voice, but I miss him because he was my partner-in-crime. Shane never gets drunk - the only time I've seen him pissed was in Glasgow last year. He hit the Scotch and was useless. Steve's a pisshead like me.
Keith, July 1996

Steve is still the favourite. He always will be. They think he's cute and lovable - sure, even I think so, so I can't blame anyone else!
Shane, July 1996

I'm very aware of what I say in interviews because I speak for Boyzone, not for myself. None of us would be able to have done this without each other, we're a democracy.
Ronan, July 1996

The lads in Boyzone are my best friends because I'm close to them and I can tell them anything. I trust them, they trust me and that's important because we spend so much time together. Everyone is there for me if anything goes wrong and each member of Boyzone has his different strengths. But we're together and that's what it's all about.
Stephen, September 1996

Ronan's completely the frontman. Without him we wouldn't have half the success we've had. Ronan holds it all together.
Shane, 1996

I was always loud and getting into silly bits of trouble, but I've had to calm myself down. I can't be selfish anymore, because what I do reflects on the others. So it's calmed me down. Made me into a nicer bloke, I suppose.
Keith, August 1996

If I was describing Keith to someone who had to meet him outside a train station or something I'd say Keith is very black and white, very plain, quite a large lad. He'll probably be wearing a baseball cap and he'll have two big wings coming out from under his cap because he's got such long hair. He'll also have a goatee and goggle eyes.
Shane, 1996

Keith and Stephen with Jamie Theakston

I have seen Stephen really angry and upset on a couple of occasions but it's pretty rare. When he gets upset he just closes up into himself, almost like a snail. I've certainly never seen him lose his temper so much that he's tried to lash out at someone.
Ronan, January 1997

I can wind (Mikey) up pretty much any time I want to. I can't remember what I said to him but the last time he threw a tantrum it was because I said something he didn't want to hear. But then afterwards we always have a laugh about it and it all blows over.
Keith, January 1997

I see Ro get all the press attention and hassle all the time and it's not what I'd want. I'm very happy to be at the back. I do what I do to the best of my ability and that's all I'm interested in. They can have their fame.
Shane, May 1997

The boys say I've changed into the person I've always wanted to be. I couldn't be this person back in Ireland. I've also learnt to see my role within Boyzone and understand what I contribute to the band.
Shane, May 1997

If I hadn't been in Boyzone I would have stayed ignorant to a lot of the ways of the world and I would have missed out. I think it's good to know about things, even if it leads me into trouble.
Keith

I think as we get bigger there's an expectation that we'll go the same way as Take That. Nearly every pop band splits after five or six years and we've been together for four, so everyone's beginning to predict it happening. And yeah, Ronan has gone way up in the popularity stakes within Boyzone in the past few months, he's gone out on his own more and people see that as an opportunity to put the band down.
Shane, June 1997

We're quite lucky in Boyzone because everyone has their funny moments, we all kinda laugh at the same things. If we're all in a daft mood, it's not easy to get us to stop messin'.
Mikey, June 1997

I admit it, I am a big softie. It's probably the way I've been raised by my mum and dad that's made me that way. I don't like to see anyone hurt, or in danger, or upset,

I feel upset with them. I just can't help it. I mean, I cry if I'm watching a cartoon and someone is killed, even though it's only a cartoon!

I tend to be quite sensitive, so when something bad happens in real life it affects me a lot. Even little things can set me off - I go all quiet and turn into myself - and I won't speak to anyone. Then I go to my room and lock myself in there.

Stephen, June 1997

I don't fight. I mean, I did when I was younger. I was in a lot of fights when I was growing up, but the important thing is it's all in the past now. In fact, I tend to steer clear of things people usually argue about. I don't take an interest in politics so I don't argue about that - I don't even know the name of the President of Ireland. As for religion, well, if people are gonna fight about religion, that that's a contradiction I itself. Religion is not and never should be about fighting.

Keith, June 1997

We've learned a lot, we've gained a lot more character. When you're younger you're very easily influenced, you're not sure what you're about. You're still learning where you're going, what you're doing. Now we've learned a bit more, who we are as individuals and we can portray it.

Ronan, October 1997

There's about a million boy bands out there isn't there? I think the public have had a bellyful of boy bands and we're all on borrowed time.

Mikey, December 1997

It's healthy to have arguments. Boyzone is like a family - you have rows with your brothers and sisters, don't you? But we try and work out our problems as soon as possible because there is no point holding a grudge. Ronan often acts as the peacemaker.

Stephen, December 1997

I'd love to be able to play the piano, more than anything. If I could buy that ability in a shop I would pay any amount of money for it just to know how to play well. I have a piano at home too, a grand piano, and I've tried writing on it but I'm just tinkling away. I want to be able to play everything!

Ronan, September 1998

I'd trust any of (the band) - not that I have any dark secrets. They know everything about me and we trust each other equally. If one of us said, 'I don't want this going any further,' it wouldn't.

Stephen, October 1998

Boyzone in general are very normal, but Mikey's really normal. He doesn't do anything extreme like the rest of us.

Shane, October 1998

The group has been successful up until now with the people who have been singing lead vocals, so I wouldn't change a thing. I've got a few of my own songs now and I'm happy with that. I did my own song on the last tour and there's more to come.

Keith, January 1999

Us Boyzone lads are still very much there for each other, but obviously we've got our things at home now, so we break away from each other as soon as we get home.

I don't know whether we'll always see each other - people often drift apart and end up living their own lives. I'm sure I'll see some of the boys, but others will do their own thing. It's like at school - you have all the best intentions of being together with your school friends for the rest of your lives, but you just grow apart. Sad as it is, it happens.

I don't think the five of us are growing apart now, though - we're just growing up. We still love each other. We used to wind each other up, but we don't any more - we just shut our mouths now. We've got enough work to do each day without upsetting each other, so we just do the gig and have a good time.

Ronan, January 1999

(Ronan)'d be rubbish as President of Ireland! As far as Ronan is concerned, he needs to get his own life and his own priorities right before he starts thinking about anything else like that.

Shane, March 1999

I think it's a shame if you're all just business partners. We hoped and dreamed we'd get this far, but we also worked very, very hard, to be honest with you. We put up with a lot of **** from a lot of people but we kept our heads down.

Keith, March 1999

(Ronan)'s good at being a TV personality and a pop star - but not a politician! I don't think he'd be the right kind of person to run a country. I don't want him making decisions for me! He's excellent at all the pop stuff, but when it comes to politics, I don't want him driving my car.

Mikey, March 1999

(Ronan)'s a great guy, but he doesn't know enough about politics. You need someone who knows what they're doing for that job!

Keith, March 1999

Keith's really funny and constantly makes us all laugh with the things he comes out with, and Mikey can be really funny too. To be honest, we've all got some comedy bits in us.

Stephen, April 1999

The best things for me is the boys. We have a brilliant relationship. In the beginning we didn't understand each other, but now we do.
Shane, May 1999

We've become more mature by living in each others' pockets around the world. We actually do still like each other. An awful lot actually, the way we've been going lately.
Keith, May 1999

If I've had a really bad time I've thought 'I can't do it today. I can't do it anymore.' It's such a demanding job and you can't just take a week off when you feel like it. But I don't think I've seriously thought that I want to go. It's just been a case of wanting to get away for a while.
Stephen, May 1999

I think because we all know each other so well, after five years of being together it's hard not to get a bit silly now and then. You don't want to mess with Stephen, though - he'll kill ya!
Keith, May 1999

I think everyone has regrets about their life, but I have none about the band. I don't regret joining, I don't regret singing any songs, and I think everything's that's happened to us has happened for a reason and it's got better and better. It's mad that after six years we can still be successful. How can I regret something like that?
Stephen, May 1999

When we do work we are friends, but we don't spend much time together apart from that. I still see Keith and Mikey socially, but we all have our own families now. Shane likes cars and I like horses.
Ronan, July 1999

Love Them For A Reason
Boyzone on the bond between them and their fans

I actually got a letter with a bunch of bananas once! The fan had read that my favourite fruit was bananas and, lo and behold, along came this letter with a whole bunch - strange!
Ronan, January 1995

A lot of (fan letters) say the same things, like 'Thanks for being there' and 'Thank you for your music'. Last night, I wrote back to some people who had sent letters to my dressing room. My mum and dad are great as well. They write back to as many fans as they can and send them the Boyzone postcards I've signed.
Stephen, July 1996

There was one time a girl sent me her bra and knickers. Now that's a fairly normal thing to be sent by a fan - but this girl had sent dirty underwear! It was actually unbelievably disgusting, because they were really dirty and all! I don't know whether she thought it was sexy, or wanted to offend me. My mother was in bits over that, I can tell you.
Keith, August 1996

I do worry very much, because a lot of fans could get jealous because I have a girlfriend, Lisa. My popularity in the band could go way down. It's alright for the likes of East 17 because their fanbase is both boys and girls, but - although we aim our music at everyone - it is mainly girls that like Boyzone. It is worrying, not just for me personally but for the band's popularity as a whole. Luckily the fans have been very good to me so far and they're been good to Lisa, thank God.
Keith, September 1996

At the end of the day, what's important is the fans. I think they know we still love them. I hope that's obvious.
Ronan, October 1996

The fans are our bread and butter. Without them, we wouldn't be anywhere. They come to the concerts, buy our albums, buy our singles. We'd be nothing without them and we give all our thanks to them.
Ronan, November 1996

I think weak-minded people could very easily get sucked in but we know the groupies want us for Boyzone, not for who we are as individuals - they don't know us. You have to understand that. We talk to people and we're civil to them but that's as far as it goes. We don't mess around.
Ronan, January 1997

The German fans are very nice people. They're an awful lot different to what Irish people or English people are.
Mikey, March 1997

I think it's terrible when you see girls sleeping on the streets just to be near us, but you can't tell them to go home, even if it's freezing, because then they think you don't want them around. You just have to accept it.

We do our best for them; I remember once when we were staying in Amsterdam and it was bitterly cold, we threw our blankets our of the window to them. I wouldn't be seen smoking or drinking too much, or taking drugs because it might upset my fans.

If I'm seen walking down the street with a girl, my fans automatically assume I'm dating, which could make them miserable. If I did get a girlfriend, I'd have to keep her very low-key, but it's easier for me not to have one.

The fans have put me where I am, so I have to give them as much as I can back. I don't understand people who make a fuss about signing autographs - it's not much to do in return, is it?
Ronan, May 1997

I'm more worried about (the fans') safety when the bus is moving. We were touring in Germany last year and just after the bus had set off we heard someone yelling. After searching for five minutes, somebody looked through the back window and saw a girl hanging on to the outside! At
that moment, the bus turned a corner and she fell off and rolled down the road. Luckily she didn't hurt herself.
Stephen, December 1997

Two years ago, we received six Smash Hits awards, which was amazing. Last year, we only received one. But this year, we're back up again. It shows that Boyzone can stand the test of time and keep doing it through all the crap. It's a real thrill. It's a proud feeling to think that the fans still want us after what we've been through - the three of us being married, two of us with kids, one with a kid on the way. It

shows that our music is definitely part of what's going on, not just our image.
Ronan, December 1998

Everyone's shown us an unbelievable amount of support this year and we hope we can continue to make you happy in the future. We've got some older fans now, but the more the merrier - everyone's welcome!
Keith, December 1998

You get a bit annoyed when (fans) are constantly outside your house, but you can't be angry with them. Even when they get hold of my phone number and stop me getting out of my front door, I never swear or anything. Sometimes I put on a deep voice, though, and pretend I'm my brother!
Ronan

Fans find me a bit intimidating sometimes. A lot of kids think I'm very unapproachable because I'm so big. But once they talk to me

they realise I'm not scary at all. People have gradually learnt that over the years.
Keith, January 1999

We've never hidden the fact that we drink a lot, or smoke, or have girlfriends and children. We haven't done it by the rules. Girls still love us even though we are married and have girlfriends. We are bigger than ever.
Keith, May 1999

I remember when Boyzone first started out, and we were on one of our very first tours. Our dressing room was next door to the room where the fans were queuing up to go in to the venue. I was sitting right up to the wall listening to what they were saying. I was amazed at how clued-up they were! They were saying stuff like, 'I'm going to sneak up to their hotel afterwards and get their autographs.' They were plotting and planning how to meet us. I was chuffed!
Stephen, August 1999

Offstage Commitments
Ronan manageing Westlife, Comic Relief, Breast Cancer charity

I've done a lot of charity work. I've taught handicapped kids drama, I used to do a lot of work with the blind. I've done a lot of charity work with the band - a lot of people write to me, and I've given stuff to the Make A Wish Foundation to be raffled. I love helping people.
Stephen, 1996

I moved into management because I like to see the other side of the coin. It helps me as an artist, it makes my job easier and it teaches me a lot. Being in management keeps my feet on the ground, because as much moaning as the pop star does, the manager works as hard and I think it's very interesting to see that.

I try to be there for the Westlife lads more than just giving them advice. They know they can always knock on my door or pick up the phone and ask, 'What should we do?' I don't want to talk down to them, I just want to help them. I was there in the studio when they were recording their vocals, though - I think that's important. Which of them is my favourite? I don't have one! I'm not allowed to.

It doesn't really worry me that Westlife might end up being bigger than Boyzone - if that happens, so be it. I want the boys to be the biggest group they can be.
Ronan, January 1999

(Westlife) are a great bunch of lads. The first time I met them I knew there was something there. I think we've found something special in the lads. There's always going to be one or two that shine more than the others but I don't know who that's going to be right now, you never really know until they get out there and get feedback from the fans and everyone else.

You can see the hunger in their eyes and the buzz they're getting, just like we had. It's just nice to be able to give someone a helping hand in the industry, like I was given.
Ronan, February 1999

We do a lot for children, cancer and Aids charities. We try and do as much as we can, especially for children - you know, we visit hospitals, do photo-shoots for charities and we're all very involved in the Make A Wish Foundation, where we visit a lot of very ill children.
Stephen, April 1999

Obviously I'd like (Westlife) to be the biggest band in the world! It's taken a lot of hard work and hopefully they'll keep their feet on the ground, but I think there's a lot of potential there.
Ronan, April 1999

Westlife

To be honest, finding the right artist to manage is what's most important in this business. You've really got to feel that you can manage that act to the best of your ability. If you team up with the wrong person it's probably not going to work out and it's unlikely you're going to have a successful band.

My side of managing Westlife is more about artistic development. The areas I look after are their music, their performance on stage, their attitudes to people on the road and where the guys are going with their look and image.
Ronan, July 1999

They haven't asked me (for a second series of *Get Your Act Together*), but at the same time, I don't think I'd do it at this stage because I've so much to do. And to be truthful, I want to be seen as a singer/songwriter. I'm not a TV presenter - it was just a bonus that I could get away with it. It's not really me, you know.
Ronan, July 1999

There's enough room for all of us in the charts. Anyway, we're six years ahead of them and Westlife have got a lot to learn. They'll be massive, but they've still got a lot of work to do.
Ronan, August 1999

Working with Disney is brilliant - as you know I was on the Hercules soundtrack and I'd love to do the voice of a Disney character. Mind you, I'm chuffed to bits to be doing the voice for a rabbit in a TV version of Watership Down. The rabbit I'll be is called Blackavar.

(The rest of Boyzone) think it's great! Loads of other talented people are doing voices of other rabbits, like Dawn French. They're even making the rabbit look like me - it'll probably have tufts of hair parted down the middle. The other lads have just said that it shouldn't be too hard for them to make me look like a rabbit!
Stephen, August 1999

The Leisure Zone
The different ways the five have found to relax from the music-biz treadmill

I need my space and some time to myself. It's how I keep sane.
Mikey, October 1995

Going to the gym is a brilliant way to relax and keep my body in shape. The more toned my body is, the happier I am with revealing all on stage.
Mikey, 1996

I'll be at home with my family - there'll be seven of us in all. Dad makes a big feast - he loves cooking the Christmas meal. He goes out and buys the biggest turkey in Dublin, so big that when I go home the next time they're still eating it. Then we go to the end of the road, to my aunt's house, and about another 30 friends and relations turn up. At some point during the day, I hope to go to church. I'd love to visit one in my parish but there will probably be lots of fans there and I don't think the priest will appreciate me signing autographs in his vestry. So I'll have to find one further afield.

I spend every Christmas at home, and it will probably be that way for the rest of my life. Everyone knows that, from the record company to my manager, Louis, and the rest of the band. There is no way I will be anywhere else. It's virtually written into my contract!
Stephen, December 1996

I like to chill by reading or watching TV. I watch films - I loved the *Star Trek* movie *First Contact*. It was excellent.
Stephen, August 1997

I've got me moods like everyone else. Sometimes I want to be with a loved one sitting on a couch watching a video, and other times I enjoy sitting on my own watching my fish. I've got tropical fish and I can watch them for ages - it just takes my mind away. I love my fish, I really do! The other day the big scavenger one ate some of the little ones and I was so worried he was going to eat the rest I didn't sleep that night! So I got up early the next morning and bought some perspex and separated him off from the others, so it's alright now, he's got his own little corner.
Shane, January 1998

I've always wanted to ride a Harley (Davidson motorbike) across America and I've still never had the chance. That would be unbelievable. I'd have to take a good few weeks off work to do it but it'll happen one day.
Ronan, October 1998

We've got a couple of horses now and Yvonne and I spend a lot of time riding them, it's really relaxing. Yvonne and her family have always been into horses, it's a real passion of ours.
Ronan, October 1998

I get up (on a Saturday) at about ten cos that's a nice time - not too early. Then I look out the back window and check my fish are still swimming happily in the fish pond. I breed Koi fish and I'm into them in a big way. Koi are very expensive so it plays on my mind all the time. I do lots of water tests to make sure the temperature's just right for them.
Shane, November 1998

I enjoy motocross. It's great bombing around the countryside in huge, four-wheel drive trucks. Sometimes I'll take a gang of mates along but quite often I'll head off on my own. I go quite a lot and it's quite good exercise to be honest. It takes the life out of you. I'll go out in the morning and drive all day.
Shane, November 1998

I catch a bit of Jerry Springer and I sometimes watch wildlife programmes on the Discovery Channel too. I'm very interested in animals, but I shoot rabbits so I don't know if I would call myself an animal lover!
Shane, November 1998

I'm definitely a winter person, it's my fave time of the year. I like staying in, walking in the rain, even going out of the cinema when it's dark and cold. I love getting into me 'jamas, putting the heating on and watching TV with a hot drink. Yup, I love winter!
Stephen, December 1998

I really love me garden. I've got a pond with some really cool fish in it. The garden takes a lot of looking after, but I don't mind, I enjoy it.
Shane, December 1998

I had a brilliant night out with (Ronan) on New Year's Eve in Dublin. We had a great time, and we kept the party going for the whole of the next day! So, no, I don't think Ronan's getting too grown-up yet.
Stephen, March 1999

We'd been together for five years and we wanted to celebrate. We thought, we can't go to a pub in Dublin and get privacy, so we decided to go to St Anne's Park, the finest park in Dublin. There were a list of rules. You could bring one or two mates, but everybody had to dress up as bin men: black hats, black boots, black coats, black trousers, so if anybody came by they'd think we were a group not to be reckoned with, and not Boyzone. They we got hungry, so we called up this Chinese restaurant. They're very exclusive and they don't deliver, but because it was us, they saw fit to do so. So we stayed there all evening, got p*ssed, played football. It was pitch black so you couldn't see the ball.
Keith, March 1999

I had various rally teams talking to me before Ford signed me up but Boyzone is a dedication for me. I could continue with just the racing career, but I would be letting four

other boys down. I'd hate to miss out on motorsport, though, so I want to keep doing both.
Shane, March 1999

I spent a week in Miami (in January) with Keith and his wife. We just chilled out, sat around by the pool and got a bit of a suntan and it was great. I love Miami, it makes a change from the miserable weather we've had over here, I can tell ya! It's important to have time to relax, so I'd lie out in the sun and read.
Stephen, May 1999

I go to places where I know I won't get hassled. I hate clubs, and if you go out to parties that are full of people in the business, people talk behind your back.
Stephen, May 1999

A lot of pop stars spend their money on wild living and cars - I prefer paintings and I drive a Peugeot 306. But I collect original Disney reproductions - I paid £9,000 for one recently. That's my biggest extravagance.
 I have a 1937 original sketch from *Snow White And The Seven Dwarves* - my house is like Disneyworld. I'm crazy about that stuff and that's my main addiction and obsession. I've got dozens of the things and they're worth thousands and thousands of pounds.
Stephen, May 1999

I just like staying in in front of the TV and having a glass of wine. I don't really go out much and I don't like nightclubs. I'd prefer to have a pint of Guinness down the pub with a couple of 60 year olds at the bar, talking about life.
 I'm quite a reclusive person and get quite tense and depressed sometimes. I found being in the public eye difficult at first and I've been very lonely. I'm not a wild person at all and I used to just come home and lock myself in.
Stephen, May 1999

I've seen The Mummy and I liked that, but we might try to go and see (Star Wars) in LA. We're all dying to see it. Actually, I should wait 'til I get home 'cos Yvonne really wants to see it as well and I might get into trouble!
Ronan, July 1999

I've just bought my ninth car! It's a 1961 red and white Chevrolet Corvette convertible and beautiful to drive. So if you see some nutter tearing around the lanes outside Dublin - that's me!
Ronan, July 1999

I haven't had the chance for months. We've just been on the Greatest Hits tour so there just hasn't been the time. I don't slob out very often, but very occasionally I like to flake out on the settee and watch films all day and nothing else.
Stephen, August 1999

Boyz To Men
The Changing image through time, plus future developements

When we first got together, none of us had the money to wear designer clothes or the knowledge to look like pop stars. Most recently, we've been able to play around with money we've never had before, and you go through changes. People start spending money on clothes or cars, but we don't want to lose where we came from.
Shane, October 1996

We're tired of wearing brightly-coloured shirts and poppy-type clothes, but it's not to build or change our audience - it's a result of us being more true to ourselves. It's not a question of trying to look older, we are older - and now we have a stronger idea of how we want to look. It's as simple as that.
Shane, June 1997

Boyzone are at a turning point as we've been here for four years. We may have started after Take That, but we're the only band left out of the old crew of us, Take That and East 17. Now we have to find out where we need to go. We want to go somewhere without alienating any of our fans, still being Boyzone, but opening ourselves to a wider audience like we did with 'Picture Of You'.

 Usually we just get dressed in nice clothes and smile for pictures. The changes are something that've been happening for a while in the band. We are starting to look older, the clothes we wear are older - maybe it's a change but it's a natural progression. If George Michael hadn't beaten us to it we'd have called the next album 'Older'.
Ronan, October 1997

We went to Bahrain and it was really hot and I wanted to get all my hair off my face. So we were on the beach and we met this little old lady who couldn't speak much English, but she offered to braid it all. The braids only lasted for seven days because it was such a quick job but I liked it so much, I got it done professionally when I got home. I love it. The only trouble is that I can't walk down a street with my hair like this because everyone recognises me.
Shane, December 1997

I think we'll regret that (Boyzone) name in four years time when we're not boys anymore. Maybe we'll have to change it to BZ or something.
Ronan, January 1998

As a group (sandals) suit the clothes we're wearing. Plus if you have a work clothes budget to spend, you might as well order a pair of Gucci sandals at £400, so you don't have to buy them yourself for your holidays! When you're travelling, getting your

socks and underwear washed is difficult, so, erm, wearing sandals gets rid of the socks problem.
Keith, September 1998

Actually, I think we looked more like farmers than schoolboys (in the 'Key To My Life' video). It's easy to laugh, but it's all part of what got us where we are today.
Mikey, October 1998

I wore (a dress) for a TV show when we dressed up as the Spice Girls. I'm worried they'll play the clip over and over again, though. I thought my white mini-dress looked very good, but the wig wasn't me. It wasn't my colour!
Ronan, TOTP special

There was an (embarrassing moment) years and years ago in Dublin where we had to wear little cycling shorts and stand in the middle of a main street. It was for 7-Up and this girl put ice down our

shorts! For the life of me, I can't remember why she had to do it.
Mikey, October 1998

I regret wearing a black over-the-knee silk dress on TV but I enjoyed doing it in the great company of the boys. Anything we've done we've done for a reason. I can never slate the things we've done because it brought us to where we are today.
Shane

I keep getting (my hair) cut, but I haven't changed the style for a while. I have had it different in the past. It was very long at one stage, then I had it really short and spiky. At one point I had it brought down over my face, and then I went back to the same style. I just think it suits me.
Stephen, April 1999

I'm becoming more prominent in the band. I have always had the ability but have never done it. A lot of people say we can't play our

instruments but I've been playing guitar for 20 years. I've just never used them in the group. It drives me mad when people say we are talentless, but I bit the bullet and it's paid off.
Mikey, May 1999

I think everybody has their own taste and the clothes I wear are basically the kind of things I like. Now and again I might wear a tracksuit when I'm around the house but most of the time I like to look smart. I feel good when I know I'm dressed decently and that's important to me. There are plenty of outfits I've worn where I just look back and think why? You don't even have to be in the public eye to do that. Everyone goes through that where you look at pictures of yourself five years ago and think, 'What was I wearing? Look at my hair! Oh my God!'
Ronan, July 1999

Me and the lads were looking back recently at all the stuff we've done and everyone was saying that I'm the only one

out of us all that hasn't changed a bit. I've still got the same hair and style for goodness sake! My face, my clothes – well I've changed my clothes obviously, but not the style of them. I'm older than Shane and Ro but, at 23, I think some of the guys look older than me (I'm not saying who!). If you do young things it keeps your mind in gear and you stay young.
Stephen, August 1999

Each new song brings a change, from 'Father To Son', to 'Different Beat', to 'Isn't It A Wonder', into 'No Matter What', which was definitely a turning point for Boyzone. We feel we've definitely catered for an older audience – if you come to any of shows now, you can see that the age group has changed dramatically. It's a proud feeling for us to see that, because it's a very difficult thing for a band in our position, a band performing pop music – a so-called boy band – to have an older audience come to our shows and enjoy them.
Ronan, 1999

Facing The Future
Together or solo? Their view

When we dont sell out our concerts, when we're not in as many magazines, that's when you know you're going down, and you can say 'Adios Amigos!'
Mikey, June 1996

I don't think I could handle it on my own. When this ends, I'll invest in property, tinker with me cars and live happily ever after. But us five lads are in it together for a long while yet and we're having the time of our lives!
Shane, 1996

I think we've learnt enough in this business that if we did want to go solo, we could. I'm sure we'll all move on to do something after Boyzone, But I think we'll stay in this business. I know myself and Ronan will.
Stephen, December 1996

When we're not hungry any more it's over for us. But there will always be someone to reach who hasn't heard a Boyzone record whether they're sitting in a house in Sheffield or South Africa!
Ronan, January 1997

If it were for the rest of my life then I'd definitely race cars. Don't get me wrong, I love my life in the band, but racing is my future. And I'd become famous doing it. It's going to be my next career. You watch.
Shane, May 1997

I don't know how far we can stick it, but I think a lot of it is down to Mikey and Keith - it's more how far they can go. Me, Steve and Ro can go on forever, 'cause it's in our blood and this is what we really want, but they have another thing to think about now - you don't know whether in a couple of years time they might say, 'Boys I've had enough, I wanna just chill with my kids.' I don't know if that'll happen and hopefully it won't, but really, the future of Boyzone is up to those two.

For me, the scariest thing of all is the thought of not being able to please our fans any more. There's always a heart-stopping moment when we release a new single, wondering where it will go in the charts. We're often asked how we feel about the success of newer bands such as the Spice Girls, but I'm not scared by that at all. It's not a competition, we do what we can to make our fans happy.
Ronan, June 1997

I can't predict the future and I don't think anybody else can. We'll just have to wait and see, I guess. I know that at some point I'll want a solo career, but at the moment I'm just really enjoying being in Boyzone.
Stephen, December 1998

(I've been) going to the studio, writing and singing - trying to get some new songs together. It's been really good, really nice. I've mainly been concentrating on songs for the whole band, but there are a few I think'd be really good for me. I've also had a go at co-producing and lots of stuff like that. Scarily enough, this is our sixth year as Boyzone, so in that time I've met up with lots of different producers, and you kind of pick things up as you go along. I can't believe that this is our sixth year - it's mad!
Stephen, April 1999

We are the most successful boy band of all time. We have been going as long as the Beatles were in the public eye. I think people forget that.

I'm sure we'll split up one day. I've got my solo single in July and I'm looking at an album next year. But Boyzone will do a fourth studio album. We're happy doing what we're doing. I want to make great pop songs. It would hurt me massively if my solo career wasn't as big or bigger than Boyzone. I'm just going to go for it and do my best.

I'm not bitter about anyone who snipes about us being a boy band. I'm a happily married man with a healthy child and people are obviously just jealous. I hear so many stories about myself. The best one was that Yvonne caught me in bed with Keith. At least I can laugh about it - although I do quite fancy him!
Ronan, May 1999

We're so lucky because a lot of the bands we started off with are now stacking shelves. I don't know what set us apart from them. We've been so lucky.

I can see us up on stage when we are 50, still doing this. We could be the new Rolling Stones. The problem is we might have to change our name from Boyzone - although it hasn't done The Beach Boys any harm. I can't see any reason why I cannot be on stage with the boys aged 55. We have discussed it and I know there will never be a farewell tour.
We enjoy it too much. I'm sure we will pursue solo paths for a while but I genuinely believe that Boyzone will be together forever.
Keith, May 1999

We had our hopes and dreams, but we never imagined we'd be this successful and last this long - fair play, it's a bonus after that.
Ronan

Everybody has a perspective that boy bands should have a life span of five or six years. Every month, there's a new story about us breaking up. But we're still together. If people want to listen to us in two to four years' time, we will still be here.
Keith, June 1999

We're taking some time out to do bits and pieces of our own, and we've got the new tour coming up in December. Ronan's releasing his solo single, I've got 'Bright Eyes' out and hopefully there will be a new Boyzone single out before the end of the year.
Stephen, June 1999

I may be doing all these other projects, but Boyzone aren't going anywhere yet. We'll carry on doing our own things but re-uniting every so often. We'll be back together in November for the UK tour.

Meanwhile, Shane is busy racing - sorry, crashing - cars. Mikey is recording his own album, Keith is hosting his own Irish TV show and Stephen's working on his solo record.
Ronan, July 1999

If the right script came along I'm sure I'd be up for (an acting career), but at the moment I wouldn't have time.
Ronan, July 1999

In ten years time I want things to be the same, but I want to be more successful internationally, with my family by my side.
Ronan, July 1999

In ten or 20 years' time, I can really imagine myself working as a film producer - but we'll have to see what happens with the singing career first!
Ronan, July 1999

There's the Boyzone movie that will be coming up next year, but also a friend of mine, BP Fallon, who has written two books about Boyzone, will be getting together with myself to write the script for another movie, but I don't want to give too much away at the moment.
Ronan, August 1999

If anything, doing solo stuff will give the band a longer life, and hopefully bring us a wider audience. Anyway, we're working on our fourth album, due for release next summer, and maybe a world tour after that!
Ronan, August 1999

I think the term solo projects can be confusing, I think individual projects is a better way of putting it. Boyzone will be a tight band for a long time.
Keith, 1999

We've just put tickets on sale for a UK tour at Christmas time. From there we're working on a fourth studio album, and maybe a movie next year.
Ronan, 1999